A PEACE OF ME

OF ME

EVOLUTION OF SPIRIT

NICOLE HALLS

BALBOA.PRESS
A DIVISION OF HAY HOUSE

Balboa Press books may be ordered through booksellers or by contacting:

Balboa Press
A Division of Hay House
1663 Liberty Drive
Bloomington, IN 47403
www.balboapress.com.au
1 (877) 407-4847

Print information available on the last page.

ISBN: 978-1-5043-2076-4 (sc)
ISBN: 978-1-5043-2077-1 (e)

Balboa Press rev. date: 02/17/2020

I will start a diary today. I am feeling somewhat empty inside, like my life force has been taken from me. This can go away. I must try and learn new ways of being. I was an addict for so long. A non believer for so long. I will try and use my value system to become a better version of myself. Yesterday held nothing incredible but nor was it nothing. I am trying to see what my heart wants. My heart needs to read the writings of Sarah again. She offered me an eternal friendship love, how amazing is that. I am currently 31 years old, I hope to live the day, I will cut down the moments of survival to hours at the moment. Also I am eating too much at the moment.

I shaved my head the other day, in absolute opposition now. Love can overcome these things though. Love is pure, light, amazing. I have felt this purity. I am needing to read her words more often, because honestly, nothing has come close to the night laying next to her. I have destroyed myself in the process of running away, and what's left? Good things, but not everything. That's ok though, I am sure things will get better with time.

I have taken a vow to never enter another relationship, because I just don't wish to hurt anyone again. I have regrets of painful things I have done, so I will try and forgive myself one day soon.

I must come back to what I know, and what I know is not much: I love my cats. I love Sarah. I can drive a car. I can eat. I enjoy cooking, a lot.

I want to create a family, that's what I wanted when I was a young child. I simply wanted to have a wife and children. Now look at me, sitting here in my singlet with no bra, tattoo's, shorts on, writing a journal about nothing. Who would have thought.

I want recovery from these mental health issues. I have been diagnosed with a few things, well I want recovery please. I am doing pretty good with my addiction issues. One leafy joint since the 28th of October. It is now the 29th November. So just on 3 weeks sober, no ciggies, no drugs, no alcohol. Feeling better for it. I have started the gym, which is great, a boxing class, which is super fun, I just realise that I have a few areas of weakness. I have been trying to get up every morning to go for a walk, but didn't this morning. The excessive sleeping is a worry for me, so I really need to try and work on that.

Work work work. I must have a meeting with someone, just to let them know that I think this job has too many triggers. I love it, but I am being triggered too much which is not working for my mental health. I am in recovery, self imposed recovery. I have had some good periods of time where I am a functioning human being, but a lot of down time too.

Recovery requires healing, emotional healing, forgiveness as well.

I no longer want to hurt myself, physically that is. To hide away from the world is more the voices' style. I know I have done wrong, and I am slowly trying to make amends, but the best I can hope for is a little better than the day before. I have some art ideas, I am very excited about the certificate 3 in visual arts, I have to complete it. That is the goal. Not just to do the work assigned to me, but to complete the whole thing. I have this great track record of starting things, doing minimal work then abandoning it. I really do wish to stick with it.

I would like to build up my ability to write again. I do love the process of writing. It is cathartic, which is so healing.

I must add, the paranoia that I used to have, like messages through the tv and music is not as bad, it still happens, but gee they are getting better. I am a human, with a spirit, not super human, in any way. I just want to be an average human being, doing average things. I know that my spirit exceeds my body, I just have to dismantle the ego. Thats where all the negative stuff is, I think.

Good evening to you all. I am here, alive. That's where I will start for now, because this building process is going to take a long time. I have to unlearn habits. I have to be strong enough to learn new ones and take photos of myself while I am at it. I am becoming, like quite literally in the process of becoming. I am sober and scared and not the greatest at taking care of myself, but again, I am alive and there is joy in that. I have met myself in some weird places. Places that bring visual images, these images are something I cannot bring myself to accept. I must bring myself to a surrender point though. I must surrender to my higher power when it comes to my destiny. I wanted to help my fellow human beings, I wanted a task that meant something. I am sure I am living that now.

Love, love, love. What to say about love. Well the woman I love is busy living her life unawares of my feelings towards her, at least that is what I think.

What other roles do I have inside me, because I have time here to learn new things. I am back at a teenage depression, sleeping in bed, stuck in my head about the woman I love, wanting to sleep all day, all night. I love playing the mother role with my two baby catlets. I am going to play unemployed for a little longer, and artist is something I need to take up more so now that I have no work. Once I remove Robert's belonging I will clean up and paint. I want to Paint so bad that it hurts my heart. But I will be on the right track, because beautiful things can come from ugliness.

That's what I need to learn how to do, bring beauty into the world, from the darkness must come light and beauty.

I am doing the best that I can, and that isn't much. I have been over sleeping. Sleeping way beyond the recommended hours of sleep a day. I have lost interest in activities that I once found fun. What's going on here? I have stopped exercising. I am eating bad foods and I cannot find the energy anywhere.

I am able bodied. I can walk and talk. I can make my own choices. I can feed myself. How do I cultivate loving kindness?

The night time gives me energy, which is annoying because I want to live the day. My mind becomes more active and kind to itself. The day is harsh critics and judgements. How can I become the person I want, or even get to know who I am if I cannot function in the necessary part of the day.

I used to write, and that release felt right, it felt natural and real. I was following a routine, now that has gone.

I am slowly coming out of a dazed and very confused time. My mood is slightly improving and my ability to wake up earlier is getting better.

When I look at pictures of friends in High School, I realise I wasn't as unpopular as I thought I was. I remember good times with these people. I remember learning new things, laughing, trying new things.

Lately I have been sleeping a lot. It seems like the best thing to do. My cats wake me up to feed them.

I had friends. I liked them and they liked me. I always thought I was shy, but I don't think I totally am shy. I think I have a mix of the introvert/extravert business happening.

What can I do to help these people in crisis? These people they are trying to destroy.

I had an idea about a mental health revolution, but that requires the truth, and the truth can hurt.

How do I seriously write about my true demons, the battle that has taken its toll on everybody around me.

I lost all my friends, all my partners, everybody around me. Why?

I have been through alcohol, pills, drugs, to kill the pain, the guilt, the SHAME. Oh the Shame. That was the biggest and hardest thing I have faced so far.

I was a religious child, I believed in God from a very young age. I knew what I wanted to be, a Mum. That is how simple it was going to be for me. I wanted to be a Mum with a chocolate baby. Now I am 31 years old, living alone with 2 cats writing about the SHAME that has plagued my life for over 13 years.

I remember as a child, looking at the TV, pointing to the ad on the screen, saying I wanted to be a Mum. There was a small African child on the TV, a charity campaigning for money for starving children. How innocent. I wanted nothing much, just the honour of becoming a parent. Something now, after all these years I could never think of doing. Am I letting the Shame win? Probably.

What does one do when your dream cannot come true? You find another dream maybe, find another goal amongst all the little things your heart wanted.

What does my heart want now?

I don't know. Maybe to be an artist. To matter. To be heard? I really don't know my sole motivation, only that love is sacred and that is my sole motivation. I wanted to be a psychologist to probably save myself. I don't think I am cut out for the study load and the necessary essay writing required in the uni life.

Dear Lord,

Hear my prayer,

I pray for myself tonight, because the fight has become a background noise. I can somewhat see some clarity here, something that has not happened in over ten years. Hear me, my tears have not fallen even though I wish they would, they are burning my eyes and my heart is aching. Hear my prayer please, I need all the light you can offer tonight. I have seen the darkness, and it wishes to envelope me. Please hear my prayers for the light is here, and I want to wrap myself up in it.

I want to wrap myself in the light. I must wrap myself up in the light.

Take from me my fears for today, help me bathe in the light today. I will transform, I will transform, I will transform.

Monday, January 1st. A new year people, something great is about to begin.

I think something wonderful is going to start happening in this world. My world is changing and I feel amazing, today. And that is totally enough, because today is all I have. I have noticed that life is a power struggle. We all compare ourselves and fight fight fight. There is another way though. And maybe I have something to add to this world. My life has been upside down. I have lived so much throughout my many years on this Earth, and I guess that means I have something to offer. There is a narrative that has plagued me, a story that has great power. I must become disciplined. I must unlearn all I have been covered in. A child's desire to protect is second to none. It was and still is my biggest weakness and strength. Weakness in the sense that I become over protective, to the point it stops the individual from reaching their own goals and moving forward with their own progression.

To comfort oneself as an adult is a difficult task, and I am speaking from personal experience. Daily, around 6:00pm I become anxious, uncomfortable within myself, so I seek movement, I seek shelter near the water, near the beach. I want to see and hear those waves crash, becoming violent with the rocks as they form the foam Kurt Cobain talks about in his song.

I have a story, like all of us.

My story for many years was shadowed, simply put, shadowed. It was my shadow playing its role within this world, and the world reflecting back at me things I have new perspectives on today. I don't feel the shame I once did, I know that shame exists, but it doesn't control me like it once did. I feel a change. A change that will, from this moment forward help me live a more authentic life. I want to incorporate daily writing into my life. I want to achieve things and sleep less. I want to learn, learn, learn. I want to be challenged and survive. I want to be creative and live a life that has meaning. I have removed sex from my life, while it was a necessary learning tool, I just cannot have it in my life. It scrambles my brain. My wires are crossed there and my relationships are not as deep and meaningful when sex is involved. Affection, beautiful and wonderful to show and is essential in our daily lives, but for me sex is a no-no. Thank you kindly to The Spirit for showing me that. Because for so long I was lost within a ghastly place, a shadow, a darkness that was too much to describe today. I am just so grateful for all that I have. I hope I can put distance between my experiences and myself. I want to develop myself I guess. If I give myself a chance, well maybe, just maybe, I can create some harmony here. There has been a narrative all along, and I have played into it very well, with all my heart to be honest, like I try and do most things I decide to do.

New beginnings. New days. New life has been granted to me, and I am absolutely, wholeheartedly grateful. If I can shine half of the light I have been given, well this could all work out perfectly ok with me.

Tuesday, 2nd January.

My eating habits have forever been an issue for me, and still they are the same. Comfort eating never stops though. What's underneath today's desire for excessive eating?

A smile can really brighten a persons day. I can speak from experience.

Do we contemplate why we are here more when we are young or when we age? Or as we age?

I want to establish well thought out patterns in my life. Smoking a cigarette after delicious food seems so counterproductive to eating. Walking with a cigarette also seems so counterproductive. What does it mean to be alive? I know I have grown. I have changed and been stagnant and been stuck and wanted to stay there. Safety in this place is hard to come by. What constitutes safety anyway? I know I once felt safe in the presence of another human being, but that isn't the way because no one else can keep me safe but myself.

I know I slept too long today, so there is some sort of grey cloud covering me at the moment, and the expression centre is out of order today.

I am craving a cigarette, but that seems counterproductive to my goal of getting strong and fit.

What are some other goals?

To gain strength, both physical and emotional strength, resilience as my Psychologist would say.

To read more, read more and learn.
Learn, learn, learn.
The ocean fascinates me, the creatures that reside in her depths.
I Reside in her depths,
To contemplate,
To resolve,

The waves carry me,
Between my shadow and hers,
Against my chest,
My heart beats,
My heart sings,
Hold on,
The wind does change,
The wind is her.
I cannot fight the sleep, the sleep, she is intense and overprotective, overwhelming.
Come forth,
Speak your name,
Quietly,
Let my eyes rest,
Let me focus,
For tomorrow will come.

I have not much to say today, but at least I have been honest and open to the world. I will have good days and bad, better days and worse, but I am free from substance and guiding myself back to the light.

January 3rd, Wednesday, wonderful and free, I am.

It seems that the narrative I was given is of great importance. The shadow side versus the light. And the light and love has won. I will never be with another human being, unless of course Sarah comes into my life. I fell in love with her very fast and very deeply. She was a woman who changed my life forever. She opened up my mind and made me feel safe. She is amazing.

The battle between light and dark, wow, what an adventure I have had. When I become stronger and my heart heals, I can really do something with what I possess. I have been blessed with much, with a great ability, with greatness, like all other human beings.

When I was young, I wanted to be a vet. Animals were my only friends. My experience found me spending my life talking to them as if they would respond. They did respond with love, companionship and gave me great joy.

The ocean, she speaks to me. When I was young all I wanted to do was a handstand, but I just didn't have enough courage to push my legs that little bit further. I was scared of death and hurting myself when I was young. It seems that I have been covered in their shadows all along. I am not saying that some were not mine, but I know all of it wasn't. I am fairly ok being alone, when I see myself as something greater than a singular something. Being isolated, I became just a part of myself, I wasn't a multidimensional person, and that is a hard place to be in. To be alone, truly alone, like mind, body, spirit, well thats a sense of hell.

Today is the 4th of January.

I have to question myself and my vessel of knowledge, or whether I have any knowledge at all. How can I be sure of anything anyway? I can feel some things in my body, so I take that as an indication of knowledge.

I am sure I saw an army man outside of my window with a shotgun, was he there to keep me safe?

Last night I used a moisturiser that reminded me of Sarah, the happy memories were amazing. My memory's are coming back slowly, enough for me not to react violently like I have.

I collapse like waves, I am naked and cold. I am here today, in this moment, intense. Greater life is a job, money, things that society require of me. I am always hungry, I don't know what for but this feeling of hunger is incessant. I cannot escape it, it eats at my soul. While I feel alone in one way, I feel connected in another. I suppose having someone near you doesn't equate to not being lonely. I know I would like to be more decisive, to make decisions and feel supported by my own inner knowing. That would feel amazing I believe.

Sometimes I write, thinking I am going to write something amazing, that need or desire to be something or someone amazing. I see the world through my eyes, and my experiences have stained my vision with both love and hate, my goal is to find that middle ground.

Where am I today? I am craving chips, hot chips. I am craving food, but I know that if I eat I will feel sick.

I compare myself, only to find myself falling very short of all others. How can I compete when we are all individuals?

Thank you kindly Spirit, for everything you have given me. I am in need of a moment of surrender, to fall at the bottom of the ocean and realise that I get lonely at home. Of course I don't want to be alone my whole life, but if I cannot believe that someone could love me, how can I be loved. No matter what someone does for me will it ever be enough. I have love, but can I find it within myself to be loved? Can I truly believe that someone could love me. That is my ultimate challenge, for today anyway.

Friday 5th January.

I felt like a cloud was covering me today. I think I am sleeping too long. I didn't wake up until 1:00pm today.

I am feeling more alive, more energised now than I was before.

Critical: you have no worth. You will never amount to anything worthy.

Nicole: What is worth anyway? Why must this worthiness involve other people. A strong opinion of oneself is a beautiful thing. An opinion that observes flaws and values, equally.

I haven't surrendered enough to trust the process Spirit has for me. I hold on to what I think I know, when what I need is flexible thinking.

Beauty, there is so much beauty in this world. People are the most amazing creatures, physical masterpieces, systems bound by there own thinking. Oh Spirit, hear me please. I am in love. I am in love with a woman and she is unaware of my feelings. She was my best friend in High School and a little beyond, but the depths of my feelings are great. My love for her is pure.

My anxiety from when I was a teenager is coming back. It comes in place of my solar plexus, and my goodness it hurts.

What of children? I am a 31 year old woman and I don't think I have ever really thought about having children. As a young girl I pointed to the TV and told my Mum that I wanted to be a Mum. And I always wanted an African American baby. I know that if I was to have a child I would want the Father to be Aboriginal. That would be amazing. A blessing.

I wish not for fortune, but riches of Spirit.

Today is the 7th of January.

I cannot settle or soothe myself. I am constantly driving around, aimlessly, thinking of things to do and places to go, and I cannot relax. I cannot think of what to write and I cannot feel a purpose. I guess I am not so ok with always being alone. I have been good without drugs and alcohol. I cannot find a spare place to lay down, a comfortable place to relax and lay down.

A time when I worked, I still didn't feel satisfied. I wanted more, what that more is though, I don't know. I am not satisfied with what I have and what I can become, I feel lost and confused. I want to surrender, but how do I even do that? I don't know what my existence is for.

What keeps me from sinking into the mighty darkness? A feeling of love, a long lost feeling of love. I have loved since, but not as pure as those days. What else keeps me a float? What roles do I play in life anyway? A daughter. A mental health patient. A consumer of services. A loner. A writer of words, incoherent jumbled mess. A Mother to Cats. Cat owner? Aimless wanderer. Consumer of goods. Infrequent gym user. Beach dweller.

The mighty darkness echoes silently between songs,

The mighty darkness desires my existence, but hold on I will, for later may be better than this moment of today.

Take me Lord, Spirit. Take me away now. Take my life with you to the depths of Hell and leave me there to breathe, if I can. I am angry and haunted, furious and haunted, did I mention I am haunted by the darkness, the darkness that I am in. I have not words but these simple expressions of the fear. I am afraid of people. I am afraid of love. I am afraid of never knowing anything. I am afraid of death. I am seeking something, something unbeknownst to me, something I cannot spell, or write into a sentence. I am angry and scared. I am sad and seething. Today is a day of nothingness, a day where I have nothing useful to do.

I have had enough for now. I surrender my soul for your purpose, so I suppose I should get used to not knowing anything. Thank you again for the many things I now have lost sight of.

January 9th today, Tuesday.

Beautiful day outside today, ugly day inside my head. I am stuck in a loop of hideousness that is controlling me. There are thoughts about killing myself, but I got this far so starting again would be pointless. Drugs and alcohol will never suffice because there just isn't enough in the world in the end, to completely rid myself of the badness. So what to do? What does one do with oneself when faced with poverty and homelessness. I guess it all depends on getting a job and having enough money to survive. I am very much faced with the prospect of being homeless and drinking myself to death or success, somehow success seems, well, almost impossible. What do I have to give the world? What has my past given me to move forward? I always wanted to help people, but here I am in a car writing. How is writing helping myself? Well it is because hopefully the feelings of hopelessness will pass and new feelings will take its place. What of being a Mother? Being a Mother? I am a Mother to my Cats, that's enough. What will you do for a job? I am giving in, but not giving up, just. I give in. Do what you will with my body and mind. I am here and I have surrendered. I am just a small pawn in your game of life and while I am aware of the greatness of the world, I am well aware of the darkness too. I take for granted so much, but I am one being. One woman, one girl, faced with so much turmoil. The girl in me is sad, she is hiding, eating in the corner, asking not to be found, but dreaming of the bigger Cole to come and find her. She is here, I am here, I am here Nicole, in the corner, in the shade, where the brick wall talks to me, it talks of its isolation too, it talks of passers by and the weather, so much about the weather. Loneliness, so much loneliness. Deep, entrenched loneliness. Now the food demon requires food. I am lonely, so lonely. I want that little Cole to feel loved. I want her to know that I would never leave her to herself, not like that, not ever. How this powerlessness feels demanding. Demanding of energy. Demanding on my knees. I am down on my knees and I cannot find a reason to get up. I thought I loved others, but I must not. If I don't love myself, how can I love others. Well I feel like I love others so much so that I am at least willing to try and love myself. No matter what I have done. I am yet to excuse some of the things I have done, but others, well thats all I knew how to do at that exact moment. I think I have changed a little since then. I guess what I am facing is loneliness here. I feel inadequate and as if I wouldn't be good company for anyone. But the thing is I don't need company all the time. These feelings of loneliness are coming from deep within, from when I was a child. There is a part of me that doesn't want to let myself slide into oblivion, to slide into that dark decay. There is no new pattern, no new habit. I find it very hard to sit with some feelings, so I drive, I drive and drink coffee, but I won't do that forever, I hope. I compare myself to everyone else. Like anyone else near me. I compare myself to homeless people on the streets, when I see them drawing and I think its better than mine. Some people might think thats stupid but I do. They are people, why couldn't they have more talent than me, just because they don't happen to have a home. What makes me a valuable citizen anyway? What kind of contribution do I need to make to feel satisfied with myself? What kind of job do I need to have? How many possessions do I need to have to be satisfied with myself? I would have thought that having a child would be the ultimate expression of oneself, but ultimately they become their own beings, something you created becomes its own entity. Where am I in that process? Being a daughter. Being a child of this world, where do I find myself on the road to wherever? I am sitting in a car, listening to waves crash against rocks, contemplating ice cream, wishing I was more productive, farting and typing at the same time. How amazing is that. But how do I share my amazing experiences? How do I find value in my own experiences? That is the key here. Maybe it is? Maybe its not. I don't know the point, nor do I know why. I have held so much inside of me that I feel like I could explode, but what to do with these expressions? Are they valid without acknowledgement? Is acknowledgement a key to our existence? Probably a key to my own existence. I have felt invisible at times, totally void of anyone knowing that I was alive. I have felt forgettable for a long long time. I have lived a forgettable life. Where my very existence has not mattered, to anyone, especially not myself. How does one formulate words into sentences to make a book about one's experience of this unique place called life. I have had the highest of highs and the lowest of lows and a mid range that could derange anyone. I have scarred my face and written on hospital walls in my own blood. I have declared war on an invisible entity, I have overdosed and survived, many times, but love.....love you say. I have been in love, been infatuated, probably still in love, but love has been the motive for it all. I am here, a free woman, typing while love wrangles its winners and losers, and I have survived. Just because love isn't returned, absolutely doesn't mean love didn't or doesn't exist. Love takes hold when it is pure. It forms an attachment to your heart, when I was young it did this, and I still cannot find a way to unleash the beauty that it attains. When love is pure, you can feel it, within and around you. Lights literally flash, the power exchange between your love and the energy, well, its something else. When love is pure she strangles the fear. When I felt love for her, my energy would radiate, my light did shine, beyond my capacity for words. I am alone but not that lonely now. I have written about her, so this note pad has been exposed to the wonder that is my love for her, Sarah.

If I ever have my dream realised of living on a boat, and I am single and alone, we all know what I will name my boat...I am a lost whale, singing my song of love, alone, forever to be alone. The magnificence of the sea shall see me rest easy one day. The sea she does not find me repulsive, she laps against my feet when I feel consumed with filth and shame. Water is my lover, for I love her and she loves me when I am drowning in shame, for that I am eternally grateful.

I have been consistent with my writing which I am completely pleased with. Now just a routine at home please Nicole. Am I lonely when I don't have things to share with others? I have a new course starting soon, how do I know this won't engage my soul? It is about art. That makes me happy. I know there are many people to thank for their support and guidance, for their helping hands and helping words. I know I couldn't have done it without them. I have been blessed, so blessed to have met these people.

When I clear myself of all these layers, who will I be? How will I cope? What will I become? Who will I become? When you lose something, something must take its place, so what will those things be? Who knew I would survive to be this age? Some Spirit knew this, and for this I am eternally grateful. I would like to contribute to this world, I just don't know how to, yet. Start small Nicole, you will find your way. Please know that I love you, and that you will be ok. Drive down the road and know that

I am with you all the way. Thank you, thank you to all the people along the way, from those I have hurt to those I may have helped. This place is magical, this place is beautiful and so are you Nicole.

I am so angry right now. My heart is hurting so bad. I want a cigarette, but that would just end and I would want another one, and on goes the cycle. My heart is hurting so badly. I feel so alone and scared about the future. How will I survive alone? People thrive and survive in relationships, they don't thrive and survive alone and sad. I want to scream and punch things. Break something. The waves are breaking with force tonight while my emotions are deep and dark. I think I am at my lowest sad moment. I have felt alone before, but not like this. I must have some strength because I don't know how I am not guzzling down wine right now. Only heal. I see that written around the place, lets just hope that it is the case. I feel helpless though. Where can I go from here. How could I possibly care about what others think of me, after all that I have been through, I am scared of what people think? So crazy! As much as the bad is here, and I surrender to the nightmare, good is everywhere, I just cannot find it in me, while I am alone. What if I had an opinion of myself that wasn't negative? What would that mean and how would I be? I want everyone to like me because I hate myself so much and I stand for nothing because everything scares me. I have poured my heart out tonight with no avail. For every cigarette a tear dries up within me. This process is unknown to me and I have to admit, its scary. It has everything to do with her, it always has and always will. Maybe I am stuck there, maybe I am not, all I know is that what it was was pure and nothing can take that away. I will use it to fight the dark because I don't I will kill myself. I don't want to, because I am scared of death. I am scared of everything. Life, death, God, people, love, truth, sadness, light, dark, everything. I don't want to scream anymore. I want to cry and lay in a ball and maybe not exist. Even people wouldn't help this feeling. No amount of hugs would eradicate this feeling. I want to crawl into my cocoon and prey. Prey to the Spirit that I am sorry and how grateful I am for the life I have lived, however shallow and unproductive. I have not achieved a degree, nor have I achieved greatness in any particular field. I have over indulged and been mean and rude and I cannot spell very well. I have smoked drugs and eaten way too much food and I don't like myself. I am so angry. Like fuming! Who am I? Who am I underneath all this? Underneath all these layers? I don't know yet, I simply don't know yet.

January 11th, My Birthday, 32 years old.

Walking isn't an issue for some, but when I feel down, I just cannot be bothered walking. When I have energy, walking is an amazing activity. I don't really know what I am doing here, and I understand that I need to question everything, but what anchors me if I do question everything? Values is my only answer. My core values. What are my core values? I am trying to find my way in this world and I am not sure I am doing a very good job. I am literally eating my way through a large amount of money and I had to lock my cats in cages this morning to hide them from the owner. I know I am processing a lot, for I cannot stop thinking. This life is mine for the taking and I am still fearful, after everything. After all that I have been through, I am still afraid. I have no real idea of who I am and what I stand for. I am a people pleaser, because I need everyones approval, because my identity is so shaky and unstable. I am blessed, don't get me wrong, I am just confused.

Dear Lord,

I am here, I exist, but what beyond that? I have fought against you for so long, and thankfully didn't win, for I know oblivion would have been the cost. Take me as I am, for I am lost and confused, hungry never, but confused, absolutely. I am a woman with a man inside of me, I am probably more man than I am woman, and more boy than I am man. There is no secret here, I am here and I exist, but why, oh why? I am 32 today and I feel spiritually weak. I don't practice anything that I should. I have an opportunity but do not take advantage of it. Sing Nicole, sing. Sing freedom songs!

These long lonely days make time seem like a disease, not the cure. I am in a backwards world where people are preying for time, I am wishing I had someone to spend time with. I don't wish it away, I simply think that I could be more productive, perhaps. I am trying to build something, God knows what. And thats the truth, because I know not what I am doing most of the time.

I have found....

I cannot blame anyone else for anything, when it is totally my way of responding that counts. I don't wish to leave this life with unresolved feelings for anyone. I want to live as authentically as possible, and I know that that involves being open to change about the people in my life, this flexible thinking, and logic. Not all my life has been tragic and difficult, I just know when the cascade of darkness falls, she falls hard and heavy, with what seems like no relief. I have had some bloody amazing friends, and people in my life. They have reflected to me that I am worthy, because they are worthy. When falling to the ground before I saw angels flying around my room, so that brings me a little peace. I used to have higher ordered thinking, now my memory is troubled. I can repair, I can rebuild and learn new things, what is stopping me? Just my own limitations. I must come to believe in Love again. I used to believe, I think, but I must realise that there has been love all along, despite the bad, Love has been there all along.

Obviously it would be stupid to completely dismiss my feelings for Sarah, because that was pure, and I learnt to push that beyond recognition, down below, somewhere where I have yet to find it again. I know the Love is there, I just have to release myself of all the layers.

Laughter is the best medicine, and children's laughter, that of angels.

Love hear me,
I am resting against these pillars,
Wounded and restless,
Forever in debt.
She is relentless,
Beauty flawless and dark,
Shadowed by imperfection,

My howls of discomfort I keep to myself.

Friday, 12th January.

I have been dreaming, so much so that I don't want to wake. My preference for sleeping and dreaming is taking over my waking world. It is really hard to motivate me out of bed. Maybe I am depressed. This is the first time since I was 14 that I haven't been on anti-depressants. Thats a big deal, now I just have to find my laughter again, and my motivation. The Sea, she sleeps softly today, waves non existent, creatures below, living their lives, quietly and cohesively. Depths; depths sing her song to me, she is magical, beautiful, soft.

God, I would love a cigarette, a joint, something to displace me from this reality. I am not enjoying myself because I am in pain, constant pain and suffering, which is probably my own fault, because Buddha says it is. What do I want? What do I enjoy? I love music, writing, the beach, singing along to songs, watching movies and documentaries, I love sport, watching and playing, what else can I love? I love taking photo's, drawing and walking. I love people but people are hard to navigate, and I am not whole within myself. If I was whole, what would that look like? How would I be different. I wouldn't let people take advantage of me, I would stand up for my rights and I would know, with my experiences what that would feel like. I must create an identity that is unshakeable, someone who is resilient, someone who takes on responsibility and uses her talents to become a woman. I am sick of wearing track pants all the time, but that is my own fault because I am overweight and I feel uncomfortable. My descent into hell was a journey of massive proportions. I don't think I am fully out of hell, I am still struggling with my shadow, which is understandable, but Spirit has touched my life, and given me insights that I know not how to express yet. I am still unsure what my role is in this life.

I must learn to let go of the past, and live in the present.

I remember thinking that if I became depressed I would get more attention. I wasn't "depressed" at the time, I was quite happy in my own little bubble of niceness. But all my newish friends had scars and war stories, and I payed attention to them, enthusiastically, so I thought, I would learn to become depressed. What a journey that has been. I have been depressed now for over a decade with numerous suicide attempts and attempts at recovery. Smoking takes our breath, it takes it away from us, something that is solely ours.

A memoir would require raw truth, an absolute portrayal of moments in my life, but which ones do I choose? I know a lot to do with shame and guilt, and those truths would be enormous to be told. I remember being young and being obsessed with sex, and even into my adult years, but there is something I must learn in all of these experiences because it has plagued me from a little girl. I remember having sexual experiences when I was in Primary school, and I wonder why this was happening? What do I need to learn from these lessons and what does writing a memoir have to do with any of it? After Kirstyn opened my world to the fact that everyone can hear my thoughts I started seeing signs, pictures that would have some sort of meaning, I just haven't learnt the meanings as of yet. Why was/is this higher power speaking to me? What can I do with all these experiences to help other people? Because deep down, thats all I have ever wanted to do. I obviously felt there were issues in the world and I wanted to help. But the funny thing was, I had all the issues that needed helping. I was the one that needed help. It took me many years to realise and confront my issues but I am on a path to recovery from whatever my combination of issues were/are.

The truth is that my truth is painful. My truth has edges when I try to swallow it. The truth is that I am ashamed at this moment in time. I used to frequent RSL's and pub's and joints that were clearly unsavoury. I met some interesting people and some not very nice people. I was so lost and lonely. I may have messed around with some men's head's but all I knew at the time was sadness and disgust for myself and my being. To feel not so lonely now, I drive around to different beaches and write and eat. I feel like the driving with music helps me process things from my life. The shame though, thats the one that wants me dead. Thats the angel that I fear. I fear shame the most and shame loves my vulnerable side because it is so weak. Enough for tonight. Thank you great Spirit.

Saturday, January 13th.

I am older but none the wiser. I am in a constant battle with the other end of the spectrum. I need to find this equilibrium. When I learn to take the negative with the positive, or those two polar opposites exist coherently together I might feel a bit more in control.

When I was living in a caravan park with my then partner, Kirstyn, I remember something happening that would forever change my little insignificant life. This event has shaken me and I would say made me a better person, in the long run. I just don't know the significance of the event and why it happened to me. And is it from the Government or God? I know the police have something to do with it, which means the government would as well. But why me? What have I done? Who am I? Why can people hear my thoughts? Why?

When I was young I believed in love, wholeheartedly. I believed in God and I believed in Love. My faith has been tested over the years, so now I find myself at a point where I question what I am going to believe in. How do I build that belief back up when so much bad has eroded my experiences of my younger years. I was looking for heaven and I lost myself in hell over the years. How do I come back to that heavenly feeling? I have doubted people and their words and actions for too long. I must find the courage to believe, not just in the something that I cannot see, touch and taste, but what I can feel. The energy. Love is an energy and deeds, actions and words that are backed by actions. Love is the greatest gift we have, and I have let it pass me by for too long. I want to believe. I am opening up my door to love and knocking down the wall that I have built and reinforced with concrete and steel. Hear my prayer great Spirit, I am coming back to love and I am bringing everyone with me. I must have a compassionate heart, an open heart, I must cultivate a strong emotional mind, build a fortress, a castle where love is stored and what I need is within those walls, because this place can be dangerous. I must give myself love and not expect it in return, a one way road of love is possible because I can learn to love myself first and not expect it back. That requires a determined mind. Sleep, it cannot overwhelm me, it cannot take my spirit. I must go to bed with the same attitude as I wake up. Love is known to me, love finds me and makes me comfortable, but I must be aware love does not Resonate with everyone and it is my job to protect myself from loveless people that are yet to come to terms with this world.

I still have to fight guilt and shame, I am far from perfect, I just got woken up a few years ago now. Love is real. Love is real.

Sunday, 14th, January.

What a wonderful day with my closest friend Chamalee. We went on a ferry to Port Arlington, ate, walked, had coffee, and it was magical. When we reached Footscray on the way home we stopped into a nice Vegetarian and Vegan restaurant, it was amazing. If I was rich I would eat there everyday. I am feeling so blessed and high on life. The universe speaks to me, that is obvious, why me is not the issue here, so I will just start to learn to take the good messages over the bad. I also saw another t-shirt today that wrote "Love wins", and you know what, it does. I know I can prey, my times of prayer are mostly not disturbed. I wrote a short story for an activity in High School, it was about how everyones pain is all equal, there are no levels of pain because that would insinuate a hierarchy, so if we looked at our pain in a way that everyone's pain was equal and to be dealt with with different strategies, different to everyone, well maybe we could get somewhere. Acknowledgement is the word I am looking for, also authenticity is also something I strive towards, a new goal of mine. For so many years I was lost within lies. A web of disastrous lies and pain and suffering. I lied to every single person I spoke to and I lied to myself. I cannot even begin to explain away the pain, but I guess I can start here and see what comes of this writing process. The water she keeps me company, I know that she will always be awake and able to listen to me. I need to believe in love again. I did so wholeheartedly when I was younger, then things covered me in emotional layers and I couldn't see myself any longer. I have done what I have thought I have wanted for a long time, to no avail. From suicide attempts to incarceration, to scars and damaged body parts, the one thing I have tried to keep a central focus on was wanting to help people. So now that I can do that, how do I do it? I am now enrolled to start a Visual Arts class, starting in late January. What if I thought of my future? I know I would love to study Art Therapy, so if I complete this course, which I will take day by day, because I know how much I love to leave something good behind, then think of enrolling in an Art Therapy course next year. Just maybe. I must start to plan for my future, somehow. A job for more income, to survive, save and earn superannuation. I don't know what will happen between now and the end of the year, I just know that I am already on my way to achieving some of my goals.

1. No cigarettes
2. No alcohol
3. No drugs
4. No sex
5. Gym

I am currently kicking number 1-4 out the door. I am taking them day by day, some easier than others, obviously. Number 5, well, a work in progress to be honest. But all good. I will get there. I have been to the depths of hell and now I can feel heaven with me on a daily basis at the moment. I am creating myself, building myself.

Through creation you will find the depths of joy and the depths of sorrow,
Face them,
For they are beautiful in their entirety,
Magnificent and Horrific,
Trust me.

Monday, January 15th.

Today I started the day with a short thought about Sarah, which is simply about love.

What am I, a Mother? A Daughter? A friend? A consumer?

I want to write something, like a memoir, but honestly looking back at the wreckage of my past, I just feel uneasy and uncomfortable.

Who am I?

I am a daughter. I don't know what I am supposed to do as a daughter. I am a friend, which is a nice role to play. I am a consumer of good and services. I am a person with thoughts and no job. I am not a woman and not a man, I just am, really.

After having a sleep I actually do something productive. But I am here, alone again and I feel slightly angry. I drive a lot, it comforts the growl of loneliness deep within, it keeps me calm but renders me useless. It's like I repeat myself, and never get anywhere new. I am starting a new course in February so that's something to look forward to.

If I was a tree what sort of tree would I be?

I would be a......

January 16th, Tuesday.

I am reading some truth from Buddha. The first card I drew was "Letting Go". It says, "let go of the memories and learn the lesson." I wonder what that lesson is? Perhaps that I am a survivor? I lived and now I can live life, fully, if I embrace a way out of the darkness into the light and love. I am a fool if I don't embrace the way to the light now. There is literally no other way to go but up from here. I have hit rock bottom, probably a few times to be honest, but I have lived in low places, places of disgust where there should be regulations about children being there.

If I was going to let go of anything I would let go of the shame. Unless I can learn all the lessons I need to, the shame can be let go I feel. The shame brings suffering, to me. How do I learn what I need to know and let it go. I need to examine it, look at it like a scientist and find a path to let it go. The "shame" consists of all the sexual memories. All the sexual encounters and things that I have done. The thoughts that I have harmed people in some way. I know I can write these memories down now, so I will begin. I don't know my age in any of these moments but I know most of them was when I was in Primary school. How would I treat a child that told me the things that I am about to write. I wouldn't scold them or make them feel as if they are strange, I would listen and reassure them that things are ok. My own punishment of myself has been a magnitude 12 earthquake. I scolded myself, I hurt myself a lot, just because I experienced sexual desire, like every other human being alive.

The best thing I have noticed lately, and that totally helps me in my recovery is people are kind to me. They make eye contact with me, or they brush past me and I don't feel like I have infected them with any disease. Eye contact is a phenomenal way of connecting with another human being.

I am trying to develop a new set of voices in my head. Like a caring parent. Someone that can help look after my needs, without judgement I guess. I wanted ice cream last night, but decided against it, especially when I want the $13.50 one.

Don't tell me your sins dear people, lets eat together and share stories of triumph. Let the sins be washed away with prayer and meditation.

I am hurting and feel annoyed and in pain. I know I have to let it go but how does one move through that. The Lords prayer talks about forgiving those that trespass against us, well I am not quite there yet. I Never even thought of it like that until I read it today and contemplated it for a serious moment. How do I forgive? I want to, I just don't know my own process yet. Writing about it helps. But are there physical actions I can take to help with the pain? I don't know the lesson of these actions, I know I need to think of life in another way, like less serious. I want to forgive, I do, not just for me.

I am beginning to feel better within myself, and use the tools that I have to become a more well rounded individual. I just know this loneliness is something to be embraced not feared.

My inner dialogue:

Cole: I want ice-cream and chips and food to comfort me.

Nicole: You cannot eat those things every time you feel discomfort. You must practice other self soothing techniques.

I do think this inner dialogue is relevant to me right now. Uncomfortable things are coming up and I am still wanting to use old habits to combat things I know I need to change.

This moment is absolutely perfect. I have gratitude for this moment, thank you great Spirit, great God and Goddess.

I exist in relation to other people. Not an individual, but in relation to my relationships.

Of course I want to matter, I want to be known and loved, who doesn't?

But if I cannot ultimately care or love myself how can I love and care for others?

Very interesting.

What of loneliness?

All I know is I experience the isolation of loneliness.

January 17th, Wednesday.

Today is Zoe's birthday, Happy Birthday Zoe.

I heard that on the wind.

The end of suffering: what are my desires? Whatever my desires, I shall find my sufferings.

Kids enjoy being comforted. And why wouldn't you, it helps to develop strong values. It is healing. To have stories for your kids is essential. How beautiful it is to tell your kid a story or tell them some kind of fact. I think that would galvanise a relationship of Mother to child, or parent to child really. I have to create the other part of my life, the better part, the positive part, where I add value to the world instead of causing suffering, to myself and others. When I was younger, I genuinely thought I was a forgettable person, that I didn't exist and that I had no value. Maybe that wasn't the truth. I know I don't matter to many, but to matter to few is better than not mattering to anyone. I truly believed as a child that no one loved me or could love me. But you see, I know now that I was created by the Spirit. And actions show the nature of the person. We have the choice to make life what we want it to be. There are strategies available to us to put us on our path. The passing cars intrigue me, where are these people going? What are they doing? I am one of those passing cars to them but I don't think they care what I am doing.

This scenery is just so beautiful. Waterfront in Williamstown. I think about Sarah a lot. She was the woman I fell in love with in High School. It was a pure love. It was pure, such a pure love. A desire to know her. Thats very important, knowing someone is the most intimate experience you can have. I cannot imagine what it's like to be married, but I am sure it would be a very pure thing.

I am capable. I am capable of doing things for myself. I didn't think I was for a long time. If I don't know about it, well I know in my heart that I can learn what it is that I don't know, or find someone who has the expertise I don't. In knowing I am capable comes a whole new range of values and skills that accompany this capability. Almost a self esteem starts to raise its head, something like trusting in ones own abilities, trusting that one can make decisions, based on what information is available at the time. What is important is knowing that though. Knowing prior to the situation that the outcome is the best possible outcome because its the only one available with the information at hand. I have so much to learn. I won't let shame conquer what I am building but I guess there is part of me that wonders why I have to give it up. As soon as I think of the reasons why, I know I have made the best decision and my shame kind of goes away. Comparison is a hard place to be. It is very hard to gauge where you are to where you want to be and who you want to be when there are so many people that you could compare yourself with. Maybe comparisons create a hierarchy? Well I think they do really. To judge yourself by the position of another creates a hierarchy, someone is different and therefore better in whatever sort of way. I loved one man, Heath, whom I fell pregnant to. I never told him and had an abortion.

One man said he loved me, I drank myself to oblivion, I became pregnant, had an abortion, and was very sick.

Love complete: purity: Sarah: eternal.

Love: male: Heath.

It is important to me to really nut through this information. Everything has been tangled for so long, I need to bring light to the darkness, let the shame feel the water, pure, sweet, cleansing. A moment in time that has frozen my heart. This fragment of a memory takes me to hell! Well at least took me to hell over around a decade of my life. Now its time to write myself out of the darkness, into the light and see what I can do with all the lessons, whatever they may be. Of course this journey has taken its time, so many days, so many years and minutes and weeks.

If I could gain the courage to face all my demons and recreate a meaningful life with pleasures that I can dedicate myself to, well then thats a bonus. Forgiveness is my key here, I don't know how to do it, I guess caring about myself is one way, well the main way. I have stopped smoking, stopped drinking alcohol, my eating habits are changing slowly, but those will be the hardest. I have comforted myself with food for as long as I can remember.

A last note, if I was to see Sarah again in my life I wouldn't want to cry, even though I might, but all I would want is to give her a massive hug. Thats all. One hug. Maybe laughter would overcome me, because it would feel like a dream come true, which it would certainly be.

I have this need to get in the car and drive, and it drives me mad. Why? What is it that I need when I go driving. It does soothe me a lot. The movement. I like the movement and the music and drinking coffee. Some days are worse than others, but today it seems that I am hard to soothe. I'm not hungry, maybe only for some sugar, but this need to keep on the move annoys me. I feel like a cigarette now as well. I must find other ways of soothing myself.

Thursday 18th January.

I am reading a writing for wellbeing book, so todays exercise is to write about what kind of tree I would be.

Happiness is the goal in life, people want to be happy. What makes me happy? What do I enjoy the most, that makes me laugh? What makes me smile? What makes me relax and enjoy myself? I don't know the answer to that question at this moment. In exchange for my love, I expect what? My love is going to waste, but can I love someone else? I don't think I can ever have sex again, that is off the charts completely for me. Today has been a bit off, I have had memories quite a bit today, not great ones, but I have survived which is always the way. But I guess the way in which I deal with these things is what matters really. My need to be centre of attention has stopped me from being a valued member of a team. I think my need for attention overrides my ability to be a part of a whole instead of trying to conquer it and call it my own. Thats ego right there. I know in my heart that I will Never see Sarah again, and that pains my heart, and makes me hurt beyond words, but she deserves love and her partner deserves love, so love it will be. I myself don't think I can be with anyone. I don't know where to funnel all this unused love I have, so I will try to find something to focus it on, because time is wasting away and I am getting older. I don't know how to be part of a team, I always want to be centre of attention because I feel so needy and unwanted. I don't know what qualities team members have but I don't think I possess them. Today is a bit of a not so positive day. I can feel the wait upon my shoulders and time is running out. Oh and don't get me started on criticism, I cannot take that, even if its constructive, I am just not built for that at the moment. Maybe one day, when I am old enough, I will have grown into an adult and I can stop one day and say to myself, you have changed, go you, Nicole, go you. If I don't have a family to leave all my stuff too, well then I leave it to someone to burn. That is it. Everything I have ever written and felt can be burnt and discarded, with my body burnt and discarded as easily as possible. I won't have family to leave anything behind to, science can have me for dissecting because I have no other use and that will probably be the best thing to happen to me, that would be the most use I would come to. Burn all my belongings, whoever has that duty. I must be realistic, I will not pass on my genes, I am way to scared of that, what if my child was to experience things like me because of me. I think science would have value from the study of me in some sort of way than any other alternative. I want to build something with all this love I have, for all the love that I have to give to the world. I cannot give her my love, so I will direct it outwards towards others and into the universe the best that I can. I am watching some really awesome DVD's at the moment, and I am learning some really amazing things. Things about our universe and people and humanity. I am also taking some positive steps to conquer some bad habits, so if, in the future I work with children, for any reason, I can be a positive role model. I can model behaviour that is possible and positive and can be emulated by them if they choose. I intend to work smart and hard to achieve some goals here on this planet. With this love I will try and build myself into something beautiful, a "beautiful mess" as Eminem says. I have a plan but who knows where life will take me, I never thought I would actually be alive at this age, I didn't think I would make it to be 32 years old. There feels like there is nowhere else to go but up now, if I let go of what I have gained, that will be a conscious choice and that's where I will stay. Trying though, I will try though. Being honest, laying out very quickly that friendship is all I can offer, because sex is gone for me and my love has been taken by a woman I will never see again. I will always remember her, and I will write her a small letter every night, but I know that seeing her and hugging her is in my dreams. Now art on the other hand, is something of great passion. If I had money I would start a collection. A goal of mine is to own a piece of art one day, a Del Kathryn Barton and Salvador Dali would be the epitome of my dreams. This beautiful warm breeze speaks to me, she says everything will be ok Nicole, you will survive and you will prosper. Learning is what you need to do, express yourself and work hard, please know this Nicole, deep within is something precious, you just cannot see it yet, you will one day, but for now lets just keep keeping on. Other people have families, I hear families where I am, so many languages, so many spheres, so many shapes and sizes, love and conversations. People fishing, people living, one person, me, writing her heart out because she has things to say. I see things, I smell things, I try hard and I have great rewards. People are amazing. Anger management for women. Anger is not a primary emotion, underneath anger there is some sort of residual emotion, that goes for men and women, so something massive is going on here and we are not living on an honest plane of existence. I need to face all my demons so I can come out the other side and help others, if I can. Music, here I come!

I am home and I cannot sleep, the night is warm so I will make the most of the bright mind.

I exist, I am alive.

Friday, 19ᵗʰ January.

I feel like I have nothing to say today, other than I am feeling quite positive, having flashbacks of moments that make me feel uncomfortable and guilty or ashamed. The way to release them it to let them come, even if they feel like they might kill you, which sometimes they feel like they will. This evening breeze is a beautiful change to today's stinking heat. I suppose I get lonely quite a bit, but I would prefer to have authentic relationships than relationships based on fear. I am talking about intimate relationships, like partners. I am not a model, nor am I even a model citizen, but I am trying now. I used to use sex as a currency, which led me down a rabbit hole of danger and darkness that nearly took my life.

It seems that tonight might be a quiet night in my mind, nothing much to ponder, nothing much to say. When I think of the enormity of some of the things I have done as a "psychiatric patient" I wonder what it all means, I wonder why I did what I did and where it all came from. What does all this mean? My thoughts go to a place of Grandeur and I think I am Jesus reincarnate, but thats just my mental illness playing up there. What is it like, not to be mentally ill? I don't know, I am trying to be not mentally ill, to be living "normally", I just don't know if I am succeeding. I am paying all my bills on time, if not early, I am learning my limits. Nikki said to be an "adult" you take on more responsibility, so how does this happen? What is responsibility anyway?

I have this innate desire to help people, and thats me assuming anyone needs help, but I found that the only person that needed help was me, and I was the only one that could save myself. What an easy job it sounds to help others, but when you think about what it takes to really change for the better, well it takes great effort.

Surrender Nicole, surrender. Be calm and stay safe for the wind blows harsh and violently sometimes, and they destroy, but you are building what you need to survive and survive you will if you surrender and let go.

You are wise and you are a fool, believe that Nicole. For moments will work out perfectly and some may fall away with great regret, just remember try with your heart and care about what you are doing. To care is to love. To care is to love. What are some of your needs Nicole?

Shelter
Food
Water
A bed
Blankets
Shower
Clothes

I write too much about nothing really. I am trying to re-birth myself, from someone who wanted to die, everyday, a shame filled creature to a human being. I don't think I will ever be annoyed by my hair again. When you didn't like who you were before can you change who you are?

Saturday, 20th January.

It seems that driving helps me process the enormity of the vast beautiful world. Today holds no special significance other than the fact that I am alive. I am alone, as what has become the norm with me, it is neither debilitating nor absolutely what I want, I guess. It falls into a place I am finding myself more comfortable with, just being sometimes. Love, when you take it on with full force, as your mantra for life, is unstoppable, impenetrable, you become fearless, everything that comes your way is something of value. Your value system becomes stronger, you believe in life again. I have been given much love in my life, and I am sure to be given more, knowing what life is like, but it is now my moment in time to give back and give love to humanity. Love is love, no matter the origin. Im unsure how to harness my love and where to direct it. I see families everywhere, it just fascinates me, having a child. How does anyone come to the knowing that they are ready to have a baby person? And how on Earth do they most often agree with someone else the terms of this arrangement. Not my place to judge, but good on them for getting to whatever place you need to be at to do that. I have no idea how to have relationships. Hence the reason I am probably alone. Daily Horoscope: Today I will find within myself something great, something worth fighting for. Love.

The good memories that are there are mind blowing, they take my breath away, they set the scene for a life of love and great fortune. Because I know I am already rich, I have fragments of gold scattered in my mind.

Sunday, 21st January.

Slowly my skills are coming back to me and I am not bombarded with sexual grossness or overload. I can be friends with people, and it asks of me nothing that I cannot give. Sex is something I cannot give, it is intertwined with too many bad memories and thoughts. But being someones friend is an amazing feeling.

I am an old tree, my root system stretches for miles, I am strong and grounded.

I am learning things, and retaining some of the information.

I am becoming more confident with going to the gym and not feeling like I am the odd one out, which is a feeling I get a lot. I remember having this feeling like I was electric blue in colour, and maybe I am but gee that was a hard period of adjustment for me. I really struggled with the messages I was receiving. The enormity of it all has decreased which is a super nice feeling, because for a moment there I thought I was going to explode with all the negativity that was going on inside me. I feel lighter somehow now, like there isn't so much negativity inside of me, and I manage to deal with it a lot better.

Great Spirit,

Please hear me today.

I have great love and great things to give, I just have yet to learn where to focus my attention. I must learn to trust you. You guided me into the dark abyss, for which I am gratefully no longer in, now where do I take what I have learnt, if anything, to bring the light to it.

I started reflecting on writing that was from like 8-10 years ago, and I could write a few things down. I think I am stupid when maybe I am just normal, and I can do normal things. I did notice that I thought myself very insignificant, which still happens, but I wonder about it sometimes. I wrote to God quite a bit, which I still do now, so our conversations haven't ceased they were just held up.

Great Spirit,

I am here to serve you but am unaware of your needs. How can I do what I was sent here to do? What do I do? I know that I must follow my values, and I must concrete those values deep within the ground. Build myself from the ground up and be brave. I must let my roots establish themselves while I work away slowly at being authentic.

Monday, 22nd January.

The time is flying and I feel like I am making slight progress on a daily basis. These goals are very important to me and my future. I feel like I could offer society something, and work hard to enjoy life, be happy and be of value. I want to be of value, not a success, as Einstein put it. I don't know what that means exactly, how you ever really know if you have been of value but I can only try my hardest. I was looking through my writing last night and found myself to be very very, I don't even know, I had or have a God complex. I don't know what the opposite of that is, being totally worthless and non existent, because I know I have felt those feelings before too. I am making good progress with the help of my friends and people that are there supporting me and we enjoy each others company. I am making friends that enjoy adventure and things other than drugs, alcohol and cigarettes. I know they are vices and I am not judging but I need a break from that, that is not all of who I am. That has been the biggest part of me so far, but I don't want it to be the only part to me. I have no idea what other roles I will play throughout my life but I want to try as many as I can. I am doing well with my goals of abstinence from things, and I am finding time for new activities and wanting more time because there is so much I would like to do.

All our cells throughout our whole body reproduce or something every 7 years to the point that everything is new. There is hope for me now. I will come to an age where the old becomes distant and the new become habit and beautiful. Because life is about love and being authentic about it, I think. I wish not to be with someone to make my loneliness go away, because that will ultimately make friction between both parties. What is love anyway? It's forms are endless and the depth boundless. I am trying and I am being rewarded with love and positive messages, and for that I am thankful. Forgiveness comes up some days, but I think I can find a way for her, she is wicked but I am me, and that means I can forgive, wholeheartedly and endlessly. I was contemplating eating meat again today and I really thought about how tempted I get, so that shows me it is something I should steer clear of. I do not want to digest an animal inside of me that once had a brain. No that doesn't feel right for me. I am finding ways to live by myself, and finding ways to entertain myself and educate myself, which is coming along lovely.

Coming to terms with the fact that my intelligence has absolutely nothing to do with anything, I would more say the desire and courage to pursue something is where it lies. If I was honest, and I am making it a priority to be so, I feel very good today. I had a great workout at the gym, a boxing class and I made a nice dinner, not too much, just enough, now I am by the beach, listening to the waves break and having a coffee. I have been able to write something thats ok over the years. I genuinely thought that everything that I ever wrote was unintelligible. And I find it is not. What little diamonds will I find? What little chucks of gold can be sifted through the filth and sex talk. I used to be funny, well at least I thought I was, which in turn made people laugh, and making people laugh used to be a goal of mine when I was in High School. That is something I should keep in mind again, connecting to people and making them laugh is a magical thing, so to work on that I need to work on my facial expressions, because I have a hardened look about me. Affection is nice, but I take it all the wrong way. I am so much better now, but I used to be quite strange with it. It seems nice when observing it in others the way they touch each other. PDA: Public Displays of Affection, well there is only so much that anyone needs to see to be honest. But nice otherwise.

Just enjoy, enjoy the ride!

Thursday, 25th January.

I need to surrender to these feelings, because I cannot do anything but feel them. There are years worth of things that I have bottled up. The goal is to survive. My brain seems foggy and I feel hungover. I am tired and I feel low. I don't know how to shift this feeling. Some days I have things to say and I can articulate myself relatively well, but today I feel terrible. I want to surrender to the feeling so it washes over me, I am stuck in the wave of this feeling. I feel like I am drowning almost. My faith in love is there, I just cannot feel the euphoria of it at this moment. I feel so angry and sad and just simply confused. I know everyone is making fun of my lack of skills and I am growing dumber by the day. I am of no value anywhere or with anyone. I don't want to exist or be alive. I want to use drugs and drink. I want a cigarette. There is a cloud hanging over me and everything I do. I am sorry but I don't know if I can do this. I cannot feel love, Lord, Spirit find me please.

I am in a forest of thieves and they want to steal the jewel of my existence, what do I do? Where do I run to? I am fearful and my energy is fading. Free me, Spirit, free me from this chase. I am sorry for my behaviour and I feel guilt about what I have done. I don't know what to do with myself, I am so scared and fearful, I am a lamb on her way to slaughter. Spirit, I cannot wake up, I am comfortable in bed, bed is where I am safe.

I am at the beach, while the waves roll with the breeze. What is it to know anything anyway? When you know something and you inform the person of some fact, what happens with that information. I really feel worthless at the moment. I feel like I have nothing to give. Do I entertain myself? I cannot write tonight.

January 27th, Saturday.

I have been in a place of self imposed darkness. I cannot quite find my way out of here. What's happening out there, in the realm of others, because inside my head I am a demon that spreads darkness across the land. I go driving, for driving helps. It comforts me and lets me listen to music. I have fallen deep again, nothing new, but different. Darker and deeper, the abyss.

Driving,
Hiding the vault,
Where darkness lies and truth shatters before me,
I drive for my life,
To satisfy time,
To alleviate shame,
To be productive without blame,
I willingly shy away from...

I have nothing new, people around me but my thoughts the same. I want to shift myself into the light. To be grateful brings light, so here I drive into that place that brings me peace. I wish for light and love for my parents, peace and happiness. Build a life from scratch like others have done. Read about others who have forged their own path in life. What would I give for a cigarette? I think it is being alone all the time, do I expect others to make me happy? Obviously I do. I cannot find it within myself to be happy for what I have. I am not satisfied? Am I ever satisfied? I want more or different or what I had or what someone else has. I am grateful for the freedom I have, the choices I have, the fear is eating away at me. I wonder why though. What could be wrong with life. I think its the thoughts of loneliness and being alone forever, even though I am only alone now. And what does that matter when you have everything you like and need and want. I know it was Tuesday's branch meeting that knocked me off my path. When I go I think that they always make fun of me, so I leave feeling terrible. My roots are fragile, and if I was a tree, I would be a sapling, planted recently, relying on the sun and rain to nourish me. Wanting to be a big tree but knowing that I was small and little and not so brave. I know that day by day I grow, baby steps for me. My mind being a harsh place to be sometimes. We all want to be noticed, maybe I wasn't given as much attention as I needed, because we are all different. People give me good and I jump away from it. What do I need to do to move forward from this habit. Because I put in my best effort with most things I do and I get positive results, I just don't believe!! BELIEVE! The universe spoke to me for years and I still have doubts, how can that be? I should be dancing everywhere I go, with everything I do. Come on Nicole! I have love to give to the world, why would I hide that? I want to change medication or completely come off this medication. I have been working on ways to take care of myself, which include good sleep patterns and not going to bed too late. Thank you for listening all.

January 28th, Sunday.

I just don't want to remember certain things, the shame is immense. I don't remember my age but I remember what happened. I feel ashamed about other events in my life. I really don't know how to forgive myself. I am lonely and ruminating, it isn't too bad, I am still alive and I haven't self harmed. I remember living by myself when I was younger, I am sure I would have died had it not been for Brodie, I am sure her presence kept me alive, and for that I thank her. Apparently God only gives you what you can handle, well I am feeling a little sensitive today. I am alive, that I am grateful for, I just don't know how to live, thats all. I have been given this greatest of gifts with no way to know what to do. I have put myself in so many negative situations that I imagine I will be living through this negativity for some time now. I have to thank Kirstyn for letting the light in, quite literally opening the blinds for me. Thank you for trying to protect me. I am never alone here. There is always people here, so I don't go insane. They have no idea their presence is peaceful to me. They come and sit and watch the water, have ice cream, talk, kids play and parents talk. Boats on the water and me in my car, dying of loneliness. I remember lying on the floor of Sarah's bedroom, safe enough to think to myself that I can think anything. Well how ever many years later, here I am, alone with my thoughts. The magnificence is something to behold, something grand and inexplainable. For so many years I wanted to destroy myself, I was out to get myself, kill myself, murder myself, now I just don't know. I want to give love but have not found the outlets for that love. I am probably still destroying myself, not looking after my body, I don't know. I notice that sometimes I look for the negative in someone else's situation to make myself feel better, but that isn't right. I want to feel good about myself because of the merit of the goodness I bring to a situation. I need to believe, how do I believe? I want to believe that I am a good person, that cares.

January 29th, Monday.

I am feeling weak at this moment. I want to throw in the exercise towel, so to speak. I am so uncomfortable in my own skin at the moment. I wonder if I have ever felt comfortable in my own skin. Maybe I have the chance to create that. My goals for not using substance are going well, I do have cravings and days where it seems like it would be easier to give in, but there is something greater at play. I know not what that is and wish not to know. I must trust in the greater Spirit more, believe that the path I am on is the path that I am meant to be on. I was never one to really think of the future, I never thought I would live this long. I wonder what I can do to improve my chances at finding a job. I wanted to be a writer when I was younger, and an artist, but I never quite found the means of expression that would help me. I don't know what to write most of the time and to try and paint, well thats a failure. I have a level of creativity I just cannot access at the moment. That's me, a juvenile sea gull, making noise to alert all other sea gulls that I am in danger, or I am hungry, but I never shut up. I seek approval with everything I do. I doubt myself all the time and I am lazy. I wonder what I could do if only I believed in myself. I give up so easily.

I am pleading with the Lord to help me. I am stretched to my limit, I want to use, but I also don't. Don't listen to me, I have lost my way. I just need to ride this wave, but how do I do it gracefully and with integrity. I am sorry for what I have done wrong. I am sorry for my actions against other people. I don't know what my authentic self looks like. She is happy, light, wearing colours, a skirt even, hippie kind of clothes, hair down, out. She is comfortable with herself, the way she looks, confident in her ability to talk to others and perform tasks that are required of her. Right now I am a child in an adults body, and that body is out of shape.

Dear Lord,

Hear this loneliness, she cries me to sleep, her voice echoes In my head, desperately longing for a message of hope. I cannot keep her away, she clings to me like a needy child, an abused child that needs love. I need love, we all need love, we just don't know how to love ourselves. With guilt and shame residing here, I am not sure anything else can grow near these things. The roots have grown deeper than I expected, I must find a way to cut these roots and draw on some strengths, whatever they may be. The clouds shift my focus, passing by like thoughts, how can I survive this place, how can I survive? I find comfort in fatty foods and rain, they both find me to be lazy and inactive, something that comes naturally to me. Find me, help! Find me somewhere, locked in a prison I built for myself, so many years ago. What can I learn from all these years of lying and deceit? Help me Nicole, Help me! Who am I? What do you want from me? I want to be free, said a mans t-shirt, well don't we all! I am scared, of course I am scared, why wouldn't my fear take over when weird stuff has been happening and I cannot find my way through the filth. This World is filled with beauty, I see it everywhere, but what of my existence? What does my existence stand for? What am I here for? I should ask myself that. The Lord gave me a chance at this game, I have to make my way through the levels. Where do I want to go? What do I want to do? What kind of person do I want to be? Shame, that is a game changer. How do I overcome adversity? Joining In might help! I am very unsure what I should do next. When I was in Rehab, I wanted to be an artist, and when I was younger I wanted to be a writer. Now I have the time to do these things, I am not using the time at all.

In the frame of mind of gratitude, nothing can really be wrong. So I take this moment to thank the Spirit for all that I have and have been given. The light breeze brushes against my legs and for that I am grateful.

January, 30th, Tuesday.

I want this love to be real. I feel like it could be but my mind gets cloudy and hazed. I don't think I have anything to say today, if only I felt comfortable, if only. I feel uncomfortable in my own skin, like I never have before, so much so that I don't want to leave the house. When I do leave the house I don't mind being out, its just the voices in my head. They are cruel and consistent and turn anything good into something bad. Do what makes me feel good, I need to do that. The waves are crashing hard today, the wind is violent in its attempts to soothe me. Sometimes I cannot tell what is real or what is fake. These voices are so harsh and life destroying. I got nothing today. I just must drive, to stay alive!

I did some guided meditation before, and now I feel a little lighter and a bit happier. I did the inner healing of the inner child. Now this could be some really important work to do. Like really important. With a patchwork memory...

A patchwork memory.

A faded well of experiences,
Jaded hallucinations
Creating waves amongst the constellations
Of my mind and not to mention,
The unmentionable shame and pain
Divided by the time I cried in public,
Oh How much I have cried in public.
Flashbacks permeate the silken walls of my office.....

I must continue to move the negative aside because the positive comes out and shines when I gently move the darkness, the shattered picture frames off the ground. There is a room, where there are many shattered picture frames, with me in them, my family, my friends. The key to pick all this up is moving slowly, gently, with protection in mind. I must trust in the ways of the land, to rest when rest is needed, sleep may not come, but that may not be the goal of the day, perhaps only rest is needed. I have been relatively authentic to my feelings lately. I know I have things of interest that I want to do and see, these things are becoming more and more prominent in my life. I must perhaps even write a list, as simple as that is, I think it may help. Thank you Spirit.

Friday, 2nd, February.

This world is so obscure to me. Do we exist in relation to how many people we know? Like the company I keep determines who I am? I am non existent here today, and I am ok with it. I don't want to be famous, or do I? My arrogance is quite large when it comes out. I should use the paranoia as fuel for the fire, rise above it and use it to become more than I am right now. I let the darkness take from me some of the essence of my personality. Maybe its just best I don't exist, and I surrender to the smallness of my life. Who knows what will come to me, lets just wait and see. I feel exhausted today. Unusually more so than any other day. I hope these new tablets work, less drowsy and I can lose weight. How do I love all parts of me? How do I turn to that part of me and let go all the shame and guilt I have expressed over the years. I need help. I don't know where I have been for the last decade, but it hasn't been a lovely place. It was cold and damp, dark, deserted, free from joy, free from laughter, I was among all the pain in the world.

Why do I have delusions of grandeur? If I truly believed I was Satan then the opposite of that would be to believe I was also the saviour. So who am I? I am Nicole, Nikki to some. But who am I? Who do I want to be? I don't really know the answer to these questions. I know I always wanted to help, but help who? Do what exactly? Who do I want to help? And who needs help anyway? Maybe my arrogance got the better of me. Of course it did, I thought I was greater than God. Who am I then? What does Nikki like? Am I a Nikki? Yes to that, I like it and thats what I want people to call me. Ok thats something sorted. What else? I like to read. I like to write. I like going for drives. I like the beach. I like basketball. I like cricket. I like footy. I am vegetarian. I enjoy coffee. I like going on road trips. I like art. I like riding a bike. I like cooking. I love music. I like movies. I like live music. There has to be something that I can do in this world to feel like a part of it. I do not wish to be famous, I don't think I would handle it that well. And there is no reason for me to be famous. I can be ordinary, I am very boring and ordinary.

I can be plain and forgettable, which I love about myself, I am totally forgettable. But what of this ego? Will it go away? And my paranoia? I must just take it day by day, like staying sober I imagine.

Darkness is not eternal, it would like you too think it was, but there is always light there. Attachment, what of that? I am attached to everyone and I would like to be less attached please world. Because I wish all to be happy and I wish all to be free. But how do we do this freedom thing? I wanted to be a Mum when I was a child, I guess that dream is over. How could I ever be a Mother after what I have experienced? I want Indigenous children. I sit alone, everyday, without fail, in my car writing a journal. It helps me process stuff I guess. To be loved is beautiful, to be understood, profound. I heard that today on Ellen. It was her 60th Birthday.

33 days without a cigarette, no alcohol, no drugs, no sex and a lot to learn. Go me!

February 3rd, Saturday.

If I was to start a dialogue between my infant self and myself, well it would be quite harsh in some respects. I know contact would be a big one. Like physical contact would be a major part of it.

I saw a woman on TV and she had a haircut like mine, she and I looked a little the same, but my point is if I think I am ugly, then I think others are ugly, which is not true. My healing process is me driving around aimlessly to the beach then home, read a little then drive somewhere else. I cannot find that sense of calm anywhere. I feel like my life is for something, but I have no idea what. Why would I have had the experiences I have if its for nothing. I feel, in this moment, that I am alive for a reason, what that is I will probably never know. If I just obey all the laws maybe something will make sense. I deeply regret so many things I have done in the past, it will take the rest of my life to heal those wounds. What is all this about? I exist in my own little bubble here, and doing what I can to keep myself safe and alive. I don't know where to turn or who I could talk to, no one in fact, except Nikki, but do I bring these things up? I surrender to the higher power, I surrender please. I cannot do anything, I feel powerless and out of control, I am just dealing with it much better than before. This being alone thing, well I guess its ok, but also not. I really want it to be authentic though. I don't wish to be with somebody if I don't feel love for them. If being alone is being authentic then being alone it must be. How do I uncover myself from all the layers I have been covered in? Because I know there is a pure being somewhere in there, before all this started and before all this became me. Kids can do anything, they believe in themselves and there isn't much covering them. I don't remember a lot. It is very destructive to my existence. I am so angry! Maybe I should go home and relax.

Sunday 4th February.

You see there is much to process. So there must be strategies for when the hunger is under control, and the money spending is under control. Although some days are so hard, other days are wonderful. I feel the breeze on the better days. I hear the birds and the waves crashing. I smile and know that I am loved and I love wholeheartedly outwards, towards the people and the world. Today is one of those processing days though, where things start to make sense, little things come together and I manage to do some things I wasn't expecting to do. I start this course in a week and I am excited and nervous, for I know not how to draw and create things. Am I strange? Unique? And if so, why? For what reason? Why am I going through what I am going through? I wonder what lessons I have learnt, if any? I underestimate myself sometimes I think. I know that living alone can send you a bit spacey, so lets just see how that goes. My place must be guest worthy at all times, what if one day I have a guest? This world is amazing and huge, beyond comprehension to be honest. Thank you for the sun today, it gave me warmth and for that I am happy.

Tuesday, 6th, February.

Today has seen me handle some negative feelings well. I am growing more confident as the days go by that I will be able to become more resilient. I know I need to work on the sleeping for so long, but one thing at a time. I am trying out forgiveness meditation, which is going ok. I am finding it hard to move through the self forgiveness part though, which is understandable. I know I need to move through these emotions slowly, so I don't lose my self like I have in the past. It seems manageable to do this and as a result love is manifesting in my heart. I knew I cared, I cared when I was young, but I lost it somewhere along the way. But I am finding my way back there. Caring and giving are the goal here. My pure love has not come back yet, I am still covered in some mud, that which is not mine. My shadow part has captured most of my existence up until now, so lets see what I can do with myself now, where the shadow isn't my whole. To restore sanity, to give me a chance at living in harmony on this beautiful planet. I used to drink to destroy myself. I wanted to die, very much. It isn't like that anymore. People and relationships are important to me. I am on a self appointed mission, but maybe not so self appointed, for everything comes from the Spirit, so a mission to move through life with love in my heart and compassion. I know not what I am here to do, I just know that it is something great. And greatness comes from within, do I really need recognition for it to be an accomplishment? I wouldn't be good with fame, I would lose myself. But I wonder about my love, the woman that has helped me, the woman that fuels my fire. I sleep too much and don't express myself too much, if at all. I loved the way she helped change my thought pattern, I thought differently because of her. How can I make something so beautiful that would express the way I have felt and would like to feel about her again. I will stick to my goals of no drugs, cigarettes, alcohol or sex. I need to move her. Move her with emotion, with love. What could I make for her? I will think about it. What would represent love? That pure love, friendship love, that comfort and heart felt caring.

Wednesday, 7th, February.

I have a name and I have the basics in life but what else do I have? My name is simple but what does it mean to me? But still, my name, I have one but where am I? Who am I? I spent a lot of time in the depths of pain, in the depths of self loathing and death, who am I now? Was I that person before? Do I matter? How do I know if I matter? I don't know, I just keep on trying and opening up my perspectives. Do I have time to work all this stuff out? I am 32 and ageing quickly, I guess, sometimes the days feel long and sleep never comes soon enough. But sleep is almost an enemy for me, I just love it. I don't know who I am, I am learning slowly but is it too slow? I feel like I want more some days, but what does that actually mean. Today is one of those days, like I want more, but what is it that I need or want? Understanding? A sudden burst of creative energy would be nice, I don't know what is holding that back, because I know I have parts of me that are majorly expressive. I need to surrender, thinking that I need to make something for someone else, or to become famous. Because I will never be famous, as if that will carve out my identity. Consistency will help me, routine will help me, confidence in those things will help me. It is hard to be consistent when my whole life has been a mess, a natural and desperate mess. No consistency, no routine, no path to be walked, just a wonderful mess. I need to pursue the meditation for forgiveness, for to let go of those things, freedom will ensue. I have a lot of potential, if only I would focus and take risks and become confident, thats all. Read your old journals please Nicole. When one loses the need to defend ones life, one can learn to feel safe. When one learns to feel safe, a personality can develop, I am at that stage now. What is important to me? What do I like to do? To eat? To wear? All these beautiful variables and endless possibilities. Focus yourself on the things that you want to learn about dear friend, learn all that you can now, you have the time and money and space. Do it. Focus your time wisely and see Things that this world has to offer. I will always be in love, that won't change, heal the sexual ills and burdens and you may face freedom. You can do this Nikki! I never knew I had a nick name in high school, I just thought I have been Nicole my whole life, but no, to my amazement I have been Nikki too, which I like. Small things amuse me, because bigger things scare me. I have been scared a lot in my life and I want that no more. I pray for you Nikki.

February 8th, Thursday, 2018.

The place I have been had no love. I couldn't love myself or anyone else. Now I must learn to care for myself, which is super hard. Is there a time of punishment, which has been the last ten years for me, but what of rehabilitation? A desire to rehabilitate? I have been in a dark loveless place, where monsters feed off every breath, feed off everything that comes into myself. Have I been tested by the devil? If so, have I passed? Everyone knew though, as if this was being broadcast to all. Well that makes me angry for a while. I know if my actions were to help somebody then it is all worth it, but I can get angry once in a while I am sure.

I don't know what is wrong with me. Since I started this course my crying has been intensified. I am already on the edge of quitting and I don't know what to do with myself. Some days are good and some days are just horrible. The horrible days are more often though. I have decided that I will talk to Ikon Institute on Monday and see about there course, then I will decide about continuing with this visual arts I am doing now. I don't really know what I am looking for. I want this amazing talent but why would it matter. I need to work on myself, healing my heart and growing up. A woman and a little boy thought I was a man yesterday, which is ok, I wasn't offended, its more to the point this is not how I want to look, at this age or ever. The negative voice is much more convincing than the golden good voice. I want long hair, straight. Brown and blonde. I know I can do some things but the things that my heart wants I cannot quite achieve, the voices and fears become overwhelming. I want to purge myself of the bad, but it always comes back, I guess its just learning to deal with it on a daily basis. When someone achieves something they would celebrate it and acknowledge it has had an impact on their lives, well I don't do that. I don't know what its like. Like for example, I still think about it sometimes I guess, but High School was a major achievement in my life. I didn't think I could do it, I acquired a drug habit in year 12 and was really starting to lose myself by the end of year 12. But somehow I made it through. I have started this course in Visual Arts, and I do really want to do it, but quitting is something I have grown accustomed to, its something I know, how do I overcome the fear associated with this adventure? You see, physical pain is something I can deal with, give me physical pain any day. I have been drug free and alcohol free for weeks now and while it feels amazing, the last week has really tested me. I didn't go down to the store one day there because I knew if I did I would buy alcohol. I rang lifeline as well, I didn't talk to anyone, and I got through it. What does all this mean? I know it has to mean something. My eating habits are terrible, but thats nothing new. Ride the wave Nikki.

I am finding when I use the expressive methods of writing or art I tend to feel much better than before I started. I have no idea why I am here, alive I mean. I know time, my time, how I spend my time is important, it matters what I do with my time. I get very confused when there are many options,

I never know what to choose. At this moment I feel like I want to do like 5 different things but am unable to make a good decision. I know that I am here to do something, whether big or small I am unaware, but something all the same. But what? I am down by the beach at night, drinking coffee, deep in thought about my parents. When I was 7 my Dad was 30 years old. That puts things in perspective. My Mum being 10 years older. I can't help but think that we all have something special to give this world, but what of recognition? What of the acknowledgement of achievements? I know not what the future will bring to me, and why I have been through what I have, I just know that right now I am feeling emotional. I want this woman to know that I love her, but what do I want in return? Is that what I am after? Something in return? Because I know that I couldn't handle anything, I am just someone learning to adult.

I once, in the not too distant past had very negative thoughts about myself, shame, so much shame. What can I say about her. Every friend I had in High School would know about "her". They, everyone for that matter knew, including her, I guess, knew I was in love with Sarah. Oh how these waves crash so heavily tonight when thinking of her experiencing pain. I think of her beautifully painted bedroom walls. The waterfall. She painted it by hand and I can remember it more than ever. She is the Queen of my heart. She loved me when I couldn't love myself and I did that for her, I believe. I hear messages of love through the songs I hear, it is a delusion I love to indulge in, it makes me happy.

This Matrix we live in makes no sense to me. I see atoms but I know nothing.

I am so confused. Lets start somewhere new today. I have to understand that I am alone here on this earth and no one is going to look after me. I have a little bit of money and the ability to work, so I am looking for a job at the moment. I have to believe in what I am doing, what I have learnt. I have to know who I am a little better. I am still starting this journey. I know I pressure myself to do things but I feel I should be able to accomplish these things. I started off strong today, and I haven't cried yet, I am just plodding along. I have good days and bad, like everyone I imagine. Thats the thing, I am growing from a child to an adult at the age of 32, better late than never I imagine. I want to start being more adventurous, but I am spending money as if I am rich. I have enrolled in a new course, a mental health course, so I can do it at my own pace for a year. Then my goal is to apply in August for next years enrolment for Social Work. I have to have goals, I have been so aimless and just let things happen with no structure or idea of what I want or where I want to go. I know I want to study, its all I have wanted to do since I came out of High School, but drugs and alcohol took me over. I am slowly learning how big the world really is. You see in a Childs development they have a stage where they believe the world revolves around them, I was stuck in that stage for a long time as an adult, displaying inappropriate behaviour. So now I am learning that I am not the centre of the world, the world is a massive huge engine that runs the way it runs with something for me to do in it, even though I am totally unsure what that thing is. I want to learn to budget and save some money so I can travel. I want to see some of the spiritual centres of the world. The waves are so calm today and I am so tired.

If I took the book I was reading seriously and wondered why I was born to the particular parents I was, well I don't know as of yet. My Mother worked hard her whole life, she was very professional, always on time and worked hard everyday she was rostered on. Self-directed recovery, well I am doing that now but I spend so much time alone that I feel like I am going mad. Again with the book, being addicted to another person, yes I was, totally. I felt something around that woman that I have never felt before. So now I must learn to gain and maintain energy another way.

There is a rhythm to my thoughts today,
They sound like Japanese calligraphy,
Peaceful strokes,
One by one.

I am constantly trying to work out where I fit into the world, and that always seems to be in relation to other people. Who am I without others? I learnt today that I am alone. I have some resources and tools, I just need to learn a few more to survive throughout the rest of my life. Time goes by so fast for everyone else, it doesn't for me, it drags on because I am so fearful. What am I to do that is worthy of this magnificent life I have been given. That's it right there. I have been given something so precious, how do I express the level of gratitude I have for what I have been given. This life is amazing, even on the bad days, but I cannot find a place to fit. I need to find that within I imagine.

Parents love to bring their children down here where I like to sit and write, and its amazing to see these little creatures that are in awe of these big people. These big people that seem to have it all together, they seem to know things and have all this knowledge that the little one wants. But little ones, they want to be big and know things, then when the time comes to knowing things, well I certainly want to be a kid again with that beautiful inquiry part of the brain working.

I am one of these adult children that has absolutely no idea what I am doing, the worst part is that I cannot fake it either, I just don't seem to know how. I know my childhood was interrupted so I must learn all these skills now as a scared adult.

I truly wish not to die with resentment in my heart or pain. I want to come to peace with all the things that have happened, that I have done and that have been done to me. I wonder if I am strong? And if I am, how do I believe that I am? How does one start to believe things? And dream? Dream of greater things to achieve? Why can I not commit to study? Have I not found the right course or is it the people aspect? Well an online course will be ok then I imagine. I know I am young and people might say I have time, but what of the time I have spent doing God only knows really. God would be, seriously, the only other person to know what I have been doing for the last 10-15 years. Dear Lord, I know not what I did, I wish for a new slate, one that allows for mistakes and the integration of past mistakes and future mistakes please. I am sure given one year, while studying that I can learn some skills of my own that could help me with my career in the health services. I am not a child whose emotions rule me, I am a woman, that can ride out the wave of emotions, thank you kindly.

Equilibrium is something that I need to learn how to achieve. Observation of emotions is something else I would like to attain. I am very harsh on myself and would like to learn how to not be so critical, because as people always say, we all make mistakes.

I love her, still. That will never change.

I build my strength with music then certain bad sexual thoughts come into my head that need to be dealt with. When I am strong enough the negativity comes, thats ok because I can mostly handle it.

I wonder what other people think about. I have always wondered that.

The truth will set you free. The world has tested me, and I am still being tested. I wonder what other people are doing? I wanted to be a mother when I was a child, I wanted to help the children on the TV. I had a simple dream, to be a wife and mother, now I sit here in the car, anxious as anything, typing my life story to nobody that will listen. To the Lord then. Because where is all this going to go? This writing is pointless and tedious and meaningless. I always break down in front of my Psychologist, always, I just seem to cry and feel terrible, I tend to forget the good days and feel bad.

Dear Lord,

I don't know what I am doing, I am repeating some old habits and gaining some new ones. I am trying my hardest to learn where I went wrong and what I must do, please forgive me for my moments of doubt, for they are great. I hear the waves now and wonder where I shall be in two weeks time, why don't I believe fully in love yet. There are moments of dislike and fear that are still there, they are just not greater than the reserves of love I am building up. I am learning so slowly that love is the answer, of which I have known all along, I just let the devil too deep. The first 30 years of my life have been a blur, it sometimes seems as if they have melted into each other with nothing much left for my memory. I am grateful, that much I know. I am grateful for the time I have had, the eternally beautiful moments of love with friends, family and animals. I have had great experiences with many people, all of which have been angels to me. People fascinate me, I want to know about people, I just can't get close enough, I falter and find myself all mixed up with words. My hair though, my physical appearance hinders my self esteem and self expression.

Dear Lord,

I still exist. I don't know when I haven't, but I have sure felt like I haven't. For many years I thought I was forgettable, so I would have sex with a man and think he would just forget about me. That didn't happen with most, I would lead them on and treat them badly, and for that I am sorry. I knew what I knew at the time and that wasn't much to do with good communication skills. Can I learn to love being alone? Like feel strong and able to support myself? I had friends when I was younger, I had really good friends, and we had some fun. Thank you all kindly for that time. One day a topic will jump out at me and I will write a book or something. If I was to pursue any art it would be writing, I do love writing a lot, drawing and painting would be a hobby. I will teach myself to paint I hope, when I can lose this anxiety.

I seem to settle at night, when the moon has come out and the day has ended, night time is definitely my time.

You see, I have given up smoking, and the reason I keep myself from touching one is to be a role model, but to who Nicole? To who my sweet? I am craving a cigarette right now.

Here are the rambles of a single mad woman. If I was to find meaning in the smallest things then I would be ok. I wouldn't feel like I have wasted a day if I could only see the funny side of the world. I used to very much see the humorous side to everything, but now I am all serious in my approach to life. I don't practice anything long enough to be good at something. I give up too soon. If I spent the same amount of time I did driving and drinking coffee I would be very good at something other than nothing. Today I am on holidays and I feel exhausted. I will go home and watch Netflix.

I am unsure what my questions are in regards to why I was born to my particular parents. What I was supposed to learn from them and that situation. Am I still healing and giving all I can to life? I ask these desperate questions to the Lord nearly everyday. What is my purpose, what is my meaning?

So I want to work really hard on my mental health issues. I now have bi-polar, and borderline personality disorder and probably other things, but I need some long term goals, some things to strive for and look forward to. I was to go on a vacation to Tasmania. I watch people smoke and I wonder why I quit. I quit because what if the strangest thing happened and I fell in love and became a mother? Would that happen in this lifetime? Who knows, I know not. The message was very clear to tell the professionals that if I was to become pregnant to get off one of my medications. Why would that information continue to come into my life. Life is strange. I feel like I am walking on a bridge, a very broken, planks of wood missing bridge, holding on to the side ropes and I am taking a step forward very slowly.

We exist in relation to others. We exist in groups, where there is a strong one, a funny one, a naughty one, the sensitive one, very interesting. Is that sociology?

So I started the first day of my forklift licence. I think I went fairly well. I drove it the best I could, no barricades down. I want to do something nice if I get my licence tomorrow, perhaps dinner and a movie, to celebrate getting it if I do. Because nothing I have ever done has been celebrated, so I must find a way to make small accomplishments something that I am proud of. If I could earn a living from doing this as a job I would be happy. You see, maybe I shaved my head because I just cannot be honest about my sexuality. The number plate today says "UUP4IT" well I think I am getting to a point where I might just be up for the challenge. I am gaining confidence so slowly, I ain't going anywhere. It seems that I have gotten over my suicidal tendency. So live I will do. But what will I do with myself? Is it hurting anyone that I sleep until 11:30? When I go to bed fairly late. I am trying to work out the dynamics here, the best way to live like a normal human being. I have rid myself of bad behaviour so why can't I stay up late and swear for that matter. It is marvellous sir, it really is. I am over the moon to be alive, I guess we just have to find that thing that gets us out of bed, the thing that we like more than being overwhelmed with depression. So maybe I will start to live. If I gain employment after this course, I would be super excited. I have never lived by myself and worked or studied, all for myself. The last time I lived alone, well Brodie basically lived with me, and bless her, because she probably saved my life, quite literally. I was struggling with prescription medication, off my face all day, every day. On the edge, daily. I was on the edge for a long time, and I am just starting to come to my senses, quite literally, with no drugs and alcohol making my senses clearer and easier to live. I smelt pot yesterday and that smelt amazing. I know that if I just don't touch it that once the cycle will not start again. Maybe I have something to offer this world, no matter how small. I know I have like a lot of love, so much love to give. I must learn to use it in the right way, because love is the most powerful tool we humans have. It, love, influences every single thing that we do, everything, no matter who you are and what you do or don't do, it all comes down to love. Whether its been a lack of love or over affection, there is never too much love, or is there? I don't think so, no. I don't mean sex in this at all. I mean caring, concerning, love.

You're immaculate,
A shining beauty,
Frozen in time,
I love you,
I cannot describe,
I simply love you,
After all this time.

What is home anyway? I have a place of dwelling, where I live, and I should clean more often, but home, what of this place? I want to step into being at home, within myself and know where I have walked for the past however many years. I want to step into some confidence, slowly learn to stand up for something. Self directed help I guess. I know I have had glimpses of self direction, and I have had levels of co-dependence. I am now out on my own, learning about the world, what the world is doing, what people are doing to each other and themselves. But what do I do with all the information that is coming into my world? I know I get anxious and I drink too much coffee, just something I need to work on.

So good news that I passed the tests. I now have the ability to drive a forklift, however scary that may be. I feel exhausted today, getting up that early for me is a real killer. I thought I had more to say today but maybe I don't. My light is waning today. I made a mistake during the test and probably nearly failed, but yeh. I cannot really think that much today. I drive because sitting down at home just causes anxiety, or my anxiety wants me to keep moving, I cannot find a way, other than to drink a million caffeinated drinks, to sooth myself down. I want to just relax and watch tv or a movie and my brain just says drive, listen to music, wait for messages. I have to not judge it I guess. You see, I have come from a dark place. If there was something for me to learn it would be..... So much. I used to like to go fishing but I don't want to kill any fish and I cannot eat them anymore. How is the sea so big that we can fish it the way we do. The world just blows my mind constantly. Its huge and amazing in the way it works, my question is, my existence? Why? The journey, the story, the path? I am someone with some sort of story, I just don't know what or how to say it. What were the experiences I have had for? For what reasons do I have some certain memories and my brain has blocked others? I want to live outside where it is warm and the weather is inviting like this. I know I ask all these pointless things and miss out on life, I guess that I just wonder about my anxiety and being unable to find a meaning for it. It enables me to come here to this beautiful place and write pointless journal entries. I guess I wonder what its all about and whether or not I can be a safe forklift driver. So weird, so weird. It is relaxing and calming typing and letting go of the things that are going on inside my brain. I want love, of course I want love, we all want love don't we. I guess I am trying to build a whole, well maintained person, whole in myself. To be authentic and real and someone with faults that don't consume her every move. I am trying to meditate every night to release and relieve some energy and paranoia. You become used to it, the paranoia. I have lived through my own kind of hell, a place so cold it hides the love and takes my memories. A place where life is not important and every move is heckled and laughed at. My pain has been all consuming, a place where no love could even begin to grow, how I survived I will never know. Maybe I would say because of Sarah. Her writings started to come back into my life when I was living with Kirstyn, and while it wasn't working with Kirstyn, my mind was beginning to see something else. I started putting Sarah's writings on my bedroom wall, and reading them and taking a message away from them, a strength. I wanted to believe in her words, I have wanted to think that my love didn't go to waste. I loved her wholeheartedly, I love her wholeheartedly. I don't know how to move on from her though, and if that is what I need to do. I am gaining strength but what do I do with the memories and the photo's? I worry about everything way too much. I must fall to my knees and prey. I must be forgiven please Lord. I must learn to let go and live wholeheartedly by myself. Thank you all, kindly.

I know I have to learn to take care of myself, I am trying to the best of my ability here. This night is so beautiful, the water is calm and the temperature is really muggy warm so feet in the water is what I did. Before I start to contemplate life again I am going to drive home.

Good day to you all. I have settled down and all the bad stuff is in my head. The world is magical and a place of wonder, but where do I fit in? And if I was more selfless would I fit into this world better? Whatever that may mean. I am learning to be selfish in a positive way, to learn how to care for myself, but my shadow is still somewhat of a monster. I have trouble around people, holding the vision of love, although I did alright at my forklift course, until I made that mistake. I lose focus easily and lose my motivation easily, the darkness takes me over and because thats what I am used too, well it seems easier to fall into that pattern. So my Psychiatrist has suggested that I take in my journal entries into my psychologist sessions to see if I can challenge some of the negative thoughts. The negative thoughts are mostly about the sexual things that I have experienced throughout my life and my self confidence when it comes to sticking things out for extended periods of time. I think maybe there are a lot more people than I was realising with negative sexual experiences, whether thats sexual abuse or sexual confusion and just not knowing what a "normal" is. Today I am feeling a bit low. I know that there is no real need to, that being alone is ok. I am still getting used to it and I guess I really need to work out whether or not I can rely on myself or not. I have managed some difficult times in the past and can navigate some difficult things, but I let myself down a lot too. I plan things then I don't follow through. I should be waiting for a few more weeks to see the positive affects of my medications.

I have had a good day. I have hung out with two friends, doing different things, and feeling included and ok about myself, in relation to other people. The waves help me think and type. I cannot seem to think and type at home. I am learning a lot on a daily basis, the lessons are just magnificent. The option of judging myself and comparing myself is a hard task not to do. I am having some memories of past events and friends and things that have happened, and it has been ok. My concern is still with work and my capabilities I guess, but we will see how I go. I know I need some new interview clothing, a nice shirt or something.

The secrets of the waves,
Singing in unison,
Splendid, magnificent in the moonlight,
Glowing highlights,
Kissing the shore, the rocks have stiffened,
I feel peaceful,
This place is heaven.

I cannot give up. I feel I could be getting stronger. My sense of humour is coming back slowly, and when that is here, I am strong. I make fun of myself and it is all good. I concentrate, I pay attention and learn. I need to do that at the Socialist Alliance meetings too because I could maybe offer something. I would like to offer something, I guess I just feel like I am not smart enough. But I have things, I have to be here on this earth for something. There has to be something I am good at and that I will have confidence in. I know I am blessed. I live in a country that is offering something to its people. There are inequalities but there are good things happening here. I need to pay attention more. I passed the test for the forklift, so if I can remember things on that, well then I can remember other things. The negative voice in my head wants to tear me down. Gee we don't give ourselves enough of a pat on the back, because I know how bad the negative voice can be, but people keep going, they keep going. Fear doesn't always win. As the waves hug the shore I am overcome with love. Goodnight to the world, to all the people I wish them all light and love.

I have noticed that when I get to my destination all the things I want to say are gone. My confidence, or lack there of is the big concern, because I don't believe in myself and my abilities to do things. I need to still learn to heal my inner child. She is wounded and alone and I don't know how to comfort her. And I don't know how to approach hobbies and things that can take up my time. I just drive around, aimlessly, and drive to the beach and write a diary where I basically talk to myself. Tomorrow I will concentrate on my resume and my booklet for the course on Friday, the order picker. I am really quite struggling at the moment, my anxiety is quite bad, I want to go for a drive but I just came back from one. I have to develop a routine of some description.

Small things are changing, my mood is definitely increasing and I am feeling much better. Things are moving slowly though, which is manageable. I still have days and moments, like now, that things aren't feeling that great, but I cannot say much really when there is a war going on and people, innocent people are dying. I don't spend much time with people because I just don't have much to say, I am not opinionated because I don't know much, my lack of knowledge makes me a target for loneliness. How do I seriously create an identity? How do I get a job when I am scared of driving the forklift. I don't want my fear to rule me but it is and does, you would think after some of the things I have seen and been through that I wouldn't be scared, but I am very scared of this world. The day light, it really isn't my friend. I feel calm at night, the night time relaxes me, the moon light calms me and my brain.

I feel like I need to cry but I am not sure what I need to release. Something needs to come out of me, I need to rid myself of something but don't know how or what. I want to scream and yell, but I cannot. I want to smoke pot so bad, but thats not adult becoming I guess. I am not sure I want to be an adult sometimes, I am not sure I am actually an adult ever really.

I think way too much about why and what for and how and whats happened. I am not sure of another approach or a way of looking at it, I am so very confused. I do have moments of grandeur, where I believe I am so good that no one is better, but on a daily basis this is not the case, I lose my energy very easily. I lose my energy with judgements, judgemental moments, where I compare myself to others and know that I am no where near where this person is. I am unemployed, just left a course, I did complete and gain my forklift licence, there are a few things happening, I just want to judge myself all the time. I couldn't even consider love, how would that even look to me anyway? What kind of a woman would want to be with me. I am not sure about that at all. I am judging again. I am trying to develop my personality, build up my strengths, believe in myself. How does one believe in oneself? I have probably rambled enough tonight, and said very little I imagine.

I know I am stuck in a rut, unable to find the courage to move. I am overly fearful and scared of my own shadow, quite literally. Does that mean that I should step out of my own comfort zone? Is that what it means when you reach a point of no return. Like I have learnt certain things and I know I need to develop and evolve but I am too scared to do anything about it. I hold myself back because I am more scared of being made fun of than a real cause. I used to be passionate and care very little about how people thought of me, now I am petrified, almost to the point, well definitely to the point of inability to really do anything productive. I want to be a productive member of society, I want to contribute something. I don't know why I have been through what I have to gain nothing from it. Hopefully one day I can do something useful. I am not sure about the position I am in right now. I guess I should just be good with my money while I don't have a job and make the best of my days.

I have lost the last two days to something undefined. I am slowly releasing my anxieties at the beach. I am getting a tarot reading tomorrow so I will see what that has to say. I am floating, somewhere in-between worlds here. I don't need anyone to find me, I need to find myself. I have many regrets and I want to make things right, so I am going to try and work towards better choices with my life. I need to cultivate more loving kindness towards people because I have hated myself for a very long time. I don't know how to rectify that situation but I will try. I know I am simple, with simple answers and simples things to say, I guess I am just not very intelligent. My ability to concentrate and focus on things is a little hard at the moment, and after the last two days, well I am just crawling back to life it feels like. I am off.

I am trying to wake myself up, from a darkness that has engulfed my life so deeply I haven't been able to see. I am trying to stay focused and not get overly emotional because I just cannot think straight. What do I want to achieve and leave in this world? I have had my time of darkness and it is now time to step into the light and build something beautiful. I am reading this book that was advised to me by the lady that did my tarot reading yesterday and it feels like it is speaking straight to me. It is insightful and informative and I want to try and adopt things from it into my life. I haven't practiced so many skills over the years, losing myself to addiction and loss of self control. I now have nowhere else to go but up and to the light. The sunlight gives its gift of warmth and guidance, and ability to see and feel things that I haven't felt for a long time. I am entangled in the light this evening, sitting in a park, relaxed and feeling love and a sense of inner peace with the breeze shifting through me.

I have to learn to be alone. To calm myself in my aloneness and be ok with it. I feel very afraid for some reason, very scared. I don't know what to think or feel, there is just a torrent of negativity happening within my mind. I cannot work anything out. I am alone and scared.

I read about something interesting yesterday about soul retrieval. How parts of your soul escape from you when experiencing trauma, to save you from the full impact of the trauma. Dissociation is a symptom of this soul loss as it is called. I believe this is what has happened to me. I know there are many things that have happened that have greatly impacted on my inability to grow and progress in life. I know right now I am not making the choices that align with the things that I value. Because I value growth and expansion, progression, but I have completely stagnated in my life. I am trying to go slowly with comforting myself better but I have started smoking again and this is stopping me from walking and exercising. I have been more in touch with nature lately which has helped me immensely. I am worrying about finding a job, so I am trying to learn how to stop worrying and let the world deliver what will be right for me. I really think a cleaning job would be ideal. I know I could handle that very well. There wouldn't be much stress and I know I like to clean, so it would be an ideal thing for me to do. I must learn to be more conscious with my money and not spend it on take away and coke but the desire for these things is immense. I will start to prey about a job I think, and hopefully something will come soon.

I am here, I exist. I am fragile, something sacred that is broken. Someone who is fearful and misunderstood. I am tired, tired of waking up to nothing. I am sure of not much, I am sure of nothing. Everything is evolving and changing and I am not fluid with that motion, I am stagnant. I don't feel refreshed in the morning after 12 hours sleep, I am tired, exhausted even. I cannot breathe, I am shaking and cold, I am lost. I don't know how to recover, I don't know where I am. Please Lord, help me. I have a lot, but I am missing much. I haven't dreamt of the future much because for so long there never was going to be a future for me. Suicide was my goal. To die, to not exist. I thought I was evil, and now I am learning I am not evil. I was mistaken, I was wrong. I am now anxious a lot. I fear a lot. I have lost many opportunities and made significant mistakes but I did not do what I thought I did. I have been taken on a deep journey and I have outgrown people. I don't feel like I belong anywhere really. Music helps, music really helps. I am lonely and alone. This constant feeling of edginess is constricting, I feel an overwhelming desire to move, to keep going, to keep doing something to distract myself from this empty feeling, this gaping massive, engulfing feeling of being worthless and unloveable. Some people are on a ship, heading to Tasmania, and I am watching that ship, slowly, glide across the water towards its destination. I am sitting in my car, craving a cigarette and company and I am alone. How will I build my confidence after these things that have happened? I don't blame these things but they have definitely affected the way I live my life currently. I believe in love, just not for me, so then do I really believe in love at all? The horizon is lit up with lights of the masses and I am alone. I don't remember what I was scared of when I was younger. The dark, because I couldn't see what was going to attack me. I am more scared than I have ever been. I am lost and also alone. I know I couldn't start a relationship with any woman, I am far too fragile and emotionally vulnerable. I don't feel like I have my life together, I feel broken. I feel like I have been shattered into a million pieces and I can't find the important pieces to put myself back together. I know silence, I know it well. I know aggression and violence well too. I don't know what I want, I never really have. I have never had direction, purpose or meaning, I have been aimless and lost. I don't know what my gift is and I want to drink myself to death tonight. Life is hard for me. Life is hard. I don't have the emotional intelligence for this place, I just don't know what to do with myself. I am so angry, hurt, broken, lost. I don't know if what I am doing with my life will change, but I know I have to actively change it if I want it to be better. The socialising part of life is hard and I am scared to do it. I don't know how to do my own hair and I am not confident in my abilities at all. I must do something, I must try something.

I have had an interesting week, well few weeks if I am totally honest. There has been a major shift in my mood, which is fantastic. I don't know if its the lifestyle changes and the consistency in taking my medication, but something has definitely been improving. I am learning to love again, let faith of a higher power, spirit, take hold, and learning about angels and archangels. I have been receiving a lot of signs, that have been allowing me to feel more secure I guess. Knowing there is something bigger out there, knowing there is good to be done. I know I have a story to tell, I guess it will come with grace and time. I just feel very good at the moment, despite being physically unwell. I have secured a good job, that pays well that can allow me to pay my bills and live more than comfortably. I can save money. As long as I keep up with my self care routines. I am only just beginning to get into the groove of this self care business, but so far it is working. And my gratitude is for my higher power, love, my angels and anyone looking out for me in prayer and thinking.

It has felt good to read books that I understand, and gain some insight into things that have happened to me in the past that I thought I was alone in experiencing. I stopped drinking so I could help myself maintain this job, because it is a great opportunity for me to learn new skills and become self sufficient. Something I don't think I have ever really experienced. I have to learn that I can rely on myself completely, that I am capable and that what I do is of value. I know there is greatness inside of me, and with the grace of my higher power I will learn where that can shine in the future. I don't know much about a lot of things, but I do know that the light within us all will get an opportunity to shine one day. There are subjects I am not ready to talk about, I am just learning to put myself in front of these situations to let the fear not be so overwhelming. I have quit smoking and drinking and I am feeling lighter and more connected to myself, my higher power and the present moment. I want to learn to pamper myself, to give myself a treat and live a little. I want to open my heart, for the love I have there is immense. It is breathtaking and beautiful. I want to let go and love. To forgive. To ask and feel worthy of receiving. This world is magnificent and I had lost that view for a long time, but through sheer, God knows what, I have survived to thrive in my own little ways.

When a story needs to be told, it will be. In time, the words will come, it will be heavenly and beautiful, magnificent like the people I have shaken hands with. I am blessed and I am absolutely grateful for everything that I have, materialistically and sentimentally. I have a lot of love in my life, I have had great love in my life. With a lot of people, with great human beings, creative, hard working human beings. And for that I am grateful. I am lost in my loving feeling, it seems wonderful to be me today. Right now, in this moment.

For now, I am taking one day at a time. Get through this sickness, become stable in work and then I could think of the future. For I would live for today, everyday, spending thousands on drugs and alcohol, cigarettes, food, just trying to dismiss the disaster of a feeling that was happening inside of me. I am learning slowly to help myself constructively.

I have stopped seeing Nikki, which is a big move. I don't know if that was her strategy, but I felt that I just had nothing else to give anymore. I have been in therapy for at least 10 years, and I need to move on and through these issues. I have coping strategies and ways to manage, I just need to put them into practice. I am eternally grateful of Nikki's help. Thank you kindly Nikki.

I am here to expel something. Something dark and deep, something universal and shallow. I need to regurgitate this essence, this darkness within. Please, Lord, Lady, help me find a way.

Dear Lord/Lady/God and Goddess,

I have sinned. It is great and I have been ungrateful. These wounds I have inflicted have been great, and I am deeply sorry. Help me please. I ask for help and forgiveness. I ask for change and challenges that I can handle. I guess I need trust more than anything I imagine. The darkness is there, it is visible and strong, but with the strength of truth and love I can fight this. I want to let go of Sarah. To find that happiness for her, in her situation. I am absolutely grateful for the time we had together, that has been my light. But to truly know that I love her, and that I am in love with her, and to know that worth, I must learn to let her go. I ask you Lord/Lady to help me reconcile this with me. I ask the angels to help with their loving guidance. I know the truth here, deep down, and I know that I am learning what I need to in my own time, and for that I am grateful. The sea she speaks to me, she whispers that love is eternal and magical in its depths. Help me fill that box with the love I have for this amazing human being, Sarah. I am so happy to be alive. Although I am alone most of the time in the physical sense, I am never alone in my heart, for she, Sarah is there. I see photos of her and still have memories and feelings of being in her presence. I can smell her too. I can see her hands playing the piano. That will never go. And for that I am eternally grateful. Thank you for the help I have had along the way. I have met some amazing people with precious hearts that are with me forever. I know I have been blessed, not just with meeting Sarah, and Cathy and Emily, but for all the true friends along the way. Thank you.

Dear God,

I am sorry. To people and to you. I have failed and I cannot find a way out of this darkness. Please help me. My heart literally hurts. Its aching and sore and it beats out of time. I have lied and cheated and hurt people. How can I find forgiveness? Please can you and the angels help me. I surrender my soul to you and your will. I have led people on so that they would love me and I haven't returned love back. I have cheated and been the cheater. I wish I was worthy of love. I wish I was worthy of her love. I don't know what I have to offer at all. I am confused and lost within myself. Here I am, but I am far. My heart beats fast and I have been tested and failed. Time and time again. I believed so deeply when I was young, but I lost it somewhere along the way. I was bombarded with lust and envy and all the sins. I had no concept of love and I hurt people because of it. That deeply pains me. I am sorry Lord/Lady, for I have sinned, and not only have I sinned I guess I enjoyed some of those sins. What does that mean for me? Redemption, is that possible? Is it possible to absolve myself of the sins of my past? Can I take responsibility for all my actions and move on? What can I create to make this world a better place? What can I give? What do I have that can help others? If you give me some more time, perhaps I can make amends with you and the people I have hurt. This distant confusion rattles between understanding and nothingness. I am lost and found in this moment. Thank you for her, Sarah.

Dear Lord/Lady, God/Goddess,

I have sinned yes, but I have also loved. Give me more time and I will love some more. We, all God's children are beautiful, we are the light. We all deserve love, no matter what. Pain is secondary to loves power. Trust me on that. I will work out a way to forgive myself for my sins, that you can be sure of. I will also learn to let go of the woman that I love, Sarah. I would never want her chained up the way I felt like she was today. I want love to liberate and free her from her fears. Give to her. Nourish her and feed her without condition.

I have learnt a lot dear Lord, and I thank you for every person I have met and will ever meet. I thank you for my parents. I will learn to realise that I have done enough. With love it is always enough. The Earth she is alive, and we must save her. I must be more conscious and stop eating meat. The remaining meat I Have I will respect with a prayer and decide to be a vegetarian again. I will find a way to let her go, I think I will compile a box of things that mean something to me, which I am doing, then burn it and put the ashes in the sea and in a hole. The elements may take my love, for she is always in my heart, where she belongs. The devil can't take the memory of my moments with her. I have abandoned my friends, and I have deep regret. I have memories but they have faded. And in this light that makes me sad. I have taken them for granted. I have spoken ill words and have spoken peoples secrets, in judgement, and for that I am sorry. In quiet reflection the revenge is living a good life without me, and that is an amazing thing, they have exercised their choice and decided I wasn't a positive force in their lives. Good for them. Thank you for the time we spent together. I did have a lot of fun, despite my moods.

If I truly believe that no one is ever going to be alone, I have to believe it for myself. I am alone physically now, but talking with my higher power. Can I handle that feeling of being alone? Trust and faith I must learn to embody. For I have broke these precious vows, to my family, my friends, my higher power. Do I still deserve love? Do I still deserve love? I believe yes. I want God to give me another chance, to give me more time, so I can make amends. So I can wash away those sins from my soul.

I feared not being loved, but I was. So much. I got some ideas to try things, to try and learn as much as I could, but I always knew in my heart I needed help. I knew I needed help, the shame was enormous, but the truth and freedom of letting the painful secret out, set me free. I truly don't believe people should be killed for choices they have made to abuse children or other people, they need help. I have no idea what kind of help they need, but help of some sort. I do believe we can make it. I do believe in love.

Thank you for the people I have had the honour of meeting. They are the light, they need to know this. Thank you for everything that has ever happened to me dear Lord, I surrender to your will. Thank you.

Joy, grief, hope, and fear are the four passions of the soul. Of these four, on which do I dwell the most? How do I understand joy and the soul? Do I create joy in my life or do I expect joy to be created for me?

I would have to say I would dwell on grief the most. I would understand joy as something of pure light. I expect it to be created for me, I would say.

Where do I encounter God? I would say God is an external force for me. In nature and animals. I have learnt in people, now that I am trying to protect myself from the pain. God is within my memory with Sarah, the love, the purity I felt for her in that moment.

Dear Lord/Lady, God/Goddess,

I am here, I exist. I am scared but I must keep going. This journey is difficult and the seas are deep. The water will save me, although I feel like I am drowning today. I have to dissect the creatures within my mind, the pain and darkness. I must expel it, now dear Lord. I ask of you for guidance and I will build my trust in you. I admit I lost faith, I don't know if I completely lost faith but faith was definitely missing from my life. I felt a pang of anger today. Time was not going quick enough, I wanted to leave work. But the music, the music helps me. There was a moment where there was no song ever written for that feeling. I couldn't even describe to you that feeling. Uncomfortable. I know I have sinned deeply and hurt a lot of people, so I must find a way to forgive myself, please give me guidance on how to do such a thing. I will let her go, with the wind and into the fire and water. I need to cleanse that love. I need to cleanse all my love. I am slowly trying to do such things. I am slowly learning things, but I know the tests will become greater and harder, I don't want to doubt myself, but that is what I am used to, so I will try and take some strategies and use them against the darkness. Expression is key, it is vital to life. Some sort of creative expression. We are all creative beings, and we need to express ourselves, we are deep beings with infinite love and wisdom. I must try and include myself in that statement and be cautious of my ego. I want to dissolve my ego if that is humanly possible. I know dancing is part of this whole thing, this challenge, and I must admit I don't know if I have ever been connected that much to my body as I would have to be to dance. I would say that feeling that moment with Sarah I was connected, definitely, but I have shut that connection to my body off very much so. Develop resilience, how is that done exactly?

Thank you for the unit I am living in, thank you for the warm bed and the water I drink. Thank you for my parents and my cats. Thank you for my friends and the time I have spent with people of my past. Thank you for the food I have to eat and the choices I can make.

Dear God/Goddess, Lord/Lady,

I must confess that I am confused as to why I have been chosen. I feel like my weaknesses outweigh the good sometimes, but I am trying to focus on love and how to let go of past mistakes. I have judged and become addicted to the darkness, but I will try now. I have seen the light and angels dance around me. The music, oh the beauty of the music. Thank you for the guidance, I appreciate the wisdom, I just know that there is something in me that needs real healing. I believe in your guidance and strength, and I am sorry for doubting you so often, even with all the love you have shown me. The family I have, the friends, the pets. I have forsaken them and let you down, so for that I need some forgiveness.

I was fearful of being abandoned, but all I have done is abandon the ones that have shown me love. For that I am sorry. I have lied and cheated and stolen peoples hearts, and for that I am sorry. I have spoken peoples secrets and spread false words about people. All in the name of fear. My fear has taken me to places where the light does not shine, well mostly. I have had doubt in the one I love. I must focus on healing now. A moment of forgiveness, a moment of peace. I must learn to smile again and share and open up my heart. I must learn to give and share love. I must heal, I must heal.

Thank you for the friends I have, thank you for my family, thank you for my pets, thank you for the food I can eat, thank you for the warm bed and roof over my head, thank you for my job and my ability to maintain my mental health, thank you for the clean water, thank you for the choices I can make every day, thank you for your wisdom and guidance, but most of all thank you for the love. The pure love.

Dear God/Goddess, Lord/Lady,

I ask for a way to forgive myself. Or at least guidance on a way. I have hurt my Mother and Father and I am sorry. I have had so much hate in my heart, it hurts me physically. I have no excuse, I have no words, I can only move forward with grace in my heart and learn to forgive myself, however that may be. The glory of your love resides in these two people, these two expressions of you. For all the pain, there is love and affection. I didn't know I didn't care. That is no excuse, no reason for my behaviour, my thoughts. I thank my Father for his time, his love of music and his dedication to his job. He rose through the ranks and became something, shared his wisdom with the world and I took him for granted. He supplied shelter and food, and gave me my first Tin Tin comic. I thank my Mum for her eternal, unconditional support, the wisdom in her ways of being and the greatness of her strength. Her dedication and hard working approach is part of the foundation upon which I walk, and for that I am eternally grateful.

I have taken so many people for granted, and thrown away their love. For that I am eternally sorry. My heart is aching and the time has come to bare my soul. I don't know exactly how to make it right yet, I don't have all the answers, I just know that if I try, slowly, to remove the sins of the past from my heart I can heal. If I can heal, anyone can heal. I prey for that healing. I send light and love to my family, my parents, my friends, my pets, the people I don't know, to all really. I don't ask for forgiveness from these people I ask for forgiveness through your grace and the strength to change the way I am. That is all, but that is everything.

Dear Lord/Lady,

The shame is heavy in my body and my heart literally hurts. I don't know how to forgive myself. I am not even sure the water could wash this off me right now. The disgrace in my eyes would be frightening I imagine. There is so much beauty in the world, I know that its there. And I don't know how long this wave will last, but am I strong enough to withstand it? Forgive me Father for I have sinned. I have taken peoples hearts and used them to create a world of hate. Music cannot help, for I do not deserve the words or melody in my ears. I do not deserve the sunshine or the friends and family that I have. These people that I have met are the glory of your kingdom, I am not. I am something beyond repair, beyond forgiveness it feels.

I imagine acceptance is the key here. I must accept all parts of myself to move on, pedophile, murderer, dictator, all these parts of myself that bring shame to the world. I have brought to the world great pain, and that is my cross to bear, I must walk with all eyes on me, to bring the world to balance. I have judged, now it is my turn to be judged. I must accept that. Thank you for your guidance, I must walk alone to find you and redeem myself dear Lord/Lady. Amen.

Dear God/Goddess,

I am not sure why I exist, but I know I want to help people. I read a message today, faith over fear, and I like this idea. I am afraid of a lot of things. I am also unsure how I can truly forgive myself. For no one is evil. And I accept that. I want to accept that I have a pedophile within my soul. I want to accept that I have a murderer in my soul. I want to accept that I have the devil and all the sins within me, because I know that I do. Help me Lord/Lady heal myself. Help me gain wisdom from the actions I have taken in the past and the thought forms within my mind. I know deep down, beyond all the darkness I am blessed, beyond words, beyond any piece of art I could ever conjure up. I have been loved and that is the miracle of life. How do I return that love? Give me the strength to do that, to show them all that I care. You have bestowed upon me a great mission, I feel honoured and fearful too. My faith will grow in time.

Please keep everyone warm.

Forgive me Father for I have sinned,

Show me the light and I will walk towards it, slowly. You have given great strength to everyone and that is a miracle to see, these people that I have met and the people that struggle, no matter where and through what shall be given warmth by your grace. Thank you for that. I am eternally grateful. Now I will let go of the woman I love, the best way I know how. With all that I do to release her into the world, and free her from my graceless heart, I ask of you, with kindness to free her heart, and mine. Thank you kindly. Eternally grateful. Amen.

This shame is incredibly thick, it stains me, my ability to think and move forward. It hurts my heart and it makes me cry. I am on my knees begging to be heard, to be forgiven, to know that everything that I have done has been for a good cause. I can never know that for sure, I can only move forward and show the love that has been shown to me. I know I have been selfish, but I care, I know that there is some part of me that cares. I take this road with increasing faith and ask of you to help me, guide me through the shame and darkness back into your kingdom of love. May I return to your kingdom?

Dear Goddess/God,

Help me with this process of forgiveness for the shame is immense. I am trying to grow, slowly, I think I am achieving something but I must admit that I am putting too much pressure on myself. I appreciate the memories that help me smile, and the shame that helps me remember the wrong I have done, for that gives me the opportunity to grow. And it seems that when I am sad or in a shameful state I can learn things. I know my eyes show my shame, and that hurts me. I wish I could see the blue when I closed them again, I started to at the hospital in Sydney. I saw the Sun and blue behind my eyes, instead of red. I want to be kind to myself, I am trying to let situations and people go. I understand that some people have decided not to talk to me, thats understandable, I appreciate their freedom of choice. I have memories that will serve me well, and you are allowing those back into my life more, so for that I am eternally grateful. And change is hard, but worth it when you see the light, or feel the light, your light, the grace that you bestow upon me. Thank you for that. You are helping me smile again with the love I have been shown by people I have had the honour of knowing. They are my angels and I have been lucky to have been raised by these beautiful people. Their strength is beyond words, their ways, unknowable. Thank you for the times I have had with them all.

The shame is intense and I feel it within me as a deep emptiness, a void, a nothingness, darkness itself. I feel it outside of me as a weight on my shoulders, so heavy I cannot stand, like in my dreams, I cannot get off my knees.

I don't know what I have done dear Lord/Lady, in all truth, in my past, I just know that the time has come for me to show love to the world. How I will do that I am sure you will help guide me. I apologise for getting stuck in fear still, my faith is growing and love is what I want, I guess this shame thing is a great force, something not beyond repair, but definitely something that should be taken slowly. Thank you for my family, my friends, my pets, my job, my unit, my bed, the warmth, fresh food, fresh water, sanitation. Thank you for all the luxuries and my ability to express myself again. I have missed that. Just like I miss my friends.

I have been blessed and I know that you are all safe and are blessed too. I have nothing more today, I am shamed and empty, and for that I am grateful and will ride the wave. Amen.

Dear Goddess/God,

I hear you In all that I do. I have reconnected with the love, your divine source of love and laughter. Thank you kindly. I have not yet achieved complete expulsion but I have great tools and armour to help me continue on my journey. Thank you for the music and the love, thank you for my family and friends, my pets and my unit and job, the food I have and clean water. When the love shines through life is perfect and I love the connection of eye contact. If I have helped one person to look into the mirror without shame, and into someone else's eyes and see that they are loved and we are all connected, well then my mission has been a success. Thank you for keeping me alive throughout this journey, I appreciate it greatly. My heart is slowly melting and filling with your grace and for that I am grateful. Help me let her go please, for she is the one I love. I will make a vow when releasing the purity of my love for Sarah, and that vow I shall keep. I will honour that until I shall no longer breathe. Thank you kindly. Send light and love to all. May we breathe in light and love and breath out darkness. Amen.

Dear Goddess/God,

Please hear my prayers. I have learnt so much negativity I cannot shake it. I am trying not to judge but I know you're testing me dear Lords. I give to you a promise to keep on this journey to find your love and my own worth and forgiveness. I know some things intellectually, but I can tell you emotionally I have yet to process these things. My heart is awakening to your love and grace and I will bear the shame and my personal cross of all the pain forever more. I will admit that it is heavy but I can feel myself growing ever so slowly in strength. I want love to prevail and I will try to build an empire out of love. Guide me please. I will ask of you no rewards, for what I have already experienced has been phenomenal. So for that I thank you. The people, oh the people I have met. The strength and kindness, the smiles, the creativity, the wonder. The hugs and smiles, the laughs and the kindness, I wouldn't give it up for anything. I have had the pleasure of shaking people's hands that may have felt low and for that I am grateful. It feels as though all I have left is love, some remnants of my past, but that is manageable, but the love, so deep, so immense.

Of course letting her go would be the right thing to do, and I will achieve that, I just need your help and guidance and grace. I know what I want but I cannot have it, so to you I give my life to help serve the people with my love. I want her happiness beyond anything else, her will being respected, her listened to and feeling safe and cared for. I want her to be warm and fed well, to have the things she needs and the things she wants, I want for her to be given love, unconditional love, love that has no parameters, no limits. I want her to be heard in every way, the depth of her soul and heart to be expressed and kept safe. Bathe her in white light and shine your heart upon her, to the depths of her being give her everything. Give her Love.

Please wash me, the caked on black tar mess that has created such fury in my eyes. Take from me the poison that has tarnished my soul and taken from me my friends and family. Take from me all that is unclean, wash it away and help me to dance. Thank you. Amen.

Dear Lord/Lady,

This anxiety is intense. I remember similar anxiety that was directed in my stomach area. I used to get severe stomach cramps, and I am starting to get them again. I am guessing that I am processing all this pain so its probably a good thing. I will continue to try and accept that. I commit my time, energy and soul to helping people, and giving up control to you my Goddess/God. Through my choices from now on I can only try to make amends for the wrongs of my past. Give to me my past mistakes please and I will try my hardest to heal the pain and bad judgements. I will come to accept my fate, whatever that may be, whatever you choose for me, I will come to accept. I will use my wisdom to make choices for the betterment of humanity, that is all there is left to do. I will let the love of my life go and give love to the world. When I get nervous at work and don't want to think about certain things, it just happens and it comes into my head. Please help me relax more. I know belief is necessary here, acceptance and belief, commitment.

Dear Lord/Lady,

I can't take any of it back, I just have to accept it, but how do I do that? How do I accept myself? Carry the weight of the pain? Think that I am helping people. I am selfish and insecure. I don't even have the words to express this pain I am feeling. I just know that people have died today and people are suffering and I am here, talking about myself, like usual. What is wrong with me? I want to purge my soul of its darkness and sing with people. Spread love and kindness. Caring about people. I forget the moments I have cared, if I have at all. There are opposites to everything, so I have to have love within me somewhere. What does that mean? What does that mean? Am I on the right track, Am I heading in the right direction? Am I where I am supposed to be? Like what is it? The anger in me is bubbling up to the surface and I don't know how to control it. I am impatient and unkind, there has to be something good within me. I would hope. Animals like me, they are a pretty good judge of character. I know I must take action, I guess I just don't know what to do. The only thing I know for sure is that I know nothing. Nothing. Darkness is here, it has enveloped me whole, I stay there, willing and still, no reflection, only thoughts. I see you all, I see the strength, I see the pain now, I see the death and I weep. Why couldn't I see what was happening in front of my face. For the love I have for you I will try and make up for it, I promise. When it gets hard, like it is right now, I will try my hardest to do my best in every situation.

Please Lady/Lord,

Help me, simply, help me here. I am kneeling here in prayer, hands gripped tight, in a moment of solitude, wondering if you could please help me. Thank you.

Amen.

Dear Lord/Lady,

I just wish I could find that purity again in all these layers. I felt it, I felt the light so many times and it is joyous to behold. The snow was pure today, so white, brilliant in its light. I can breathe that in. I woke up with Sarah on my mind and a boat, with fresh glowing blue water in the background, thank you for that.

I know the hardest things are teaching me the greatest things, I guess I just need to keep fighting the good fight. To keep on going. You have given me guiding angels throughout my life and I feel blessed for that. Thank you for their gifts of strength and wisdom. I haven't listened to so many people. Please send light and love to all human beings, animals. Thank you for your gifts.

Amen.

Dear Lady/Lord,

Thank you for listening to my words and giving me guidance. I hope to be a Mother one day and I give my praise to those who have given me the joy of witnessing life in action.

Please hear me Lord/Lady,

You have given me pure love with a woman that I will never forget, nor will I ever move past that. It was Love in its purest form and for that I am completely and utterly eternally grateful. I hand over my willingness and acceptance of my grand situation if you help me let her go. Give to me the gift of that and I am your servant, and the worlds servant over again. Find within me purity and light, for she, Sarah, is my all. I will honour thoughts of her with actions of Love, and I will listen to music with the divine knowledge that she is always with me. She, Sarah, is within my heart and soul and I have had the pleasure and honour of knowing her, even a little, listening to her voice, seeing her smile and hearing her laugh. And that is the gift I will die with, so thank you and I thank her with the depth of my being. I hope her heart is safe and warm, nestled within a nest of twigs and leaves, a soft place for her to find peace, where she can breathe in the light and breathe out the darkness tenderly for eternity.

Thank you for the warmth of the Sun, and the Love of my family.

There is value within each of us, and that is how we change how society controls us. We stand up and claim our story, with bravery and breath. We find the creativity that expresses our worth, we encourage ourselves and others to pursue our dreams and we do it. We simply do it. We distribute the wealth by claiming it. We claim our share by expressing ourselves and inspiring others with what is us, our strength and light.

Don't give up on me Lord/Lady, for I have been given the greatest gift and that is to see strength and light. I must let the past go, what's done is done and forgiveness will come, but I am seeing strength and light in all those that I see. We cannot keep covering our children in dark matter, in the darkness that was handed down to us, we must give them light and love and safety.

I know this World can change and it is and it will continue to do so, we will just give it time, for there is so much time, so much time for Love to prevail.

I am blessed, completely blessed and I wish for that blessing to be passed on to all my fellow human beings and animals and creatures great and small. The value is within us. Let's express it, myself included.

I wish for World Peace, I wish for Love to prevail. I know it can, I will help if I can, that much I know.

Thank you for listening to me and thank you for the rainbows. Thank you for the music and thank you for the people. Thank you for the animals and thank you for the food. You have created something phenomenal here and I know, with certainty, that Love is the answer.

Thank you for Love.

Amen.

Dear Lady/Lord,

I have come to this World for a reason unbeknownst to myself, and I take from you, my higher power the guidance and wisdom to know that whatever you have planned is what must be. I am trying to leave the past in the past but it is very hard, it takes my attention from me at times. I want to learn new things but I am falling into a pattern at work where I am doing what I am comfortable doing. I don't want that. I want to evolve. Please help me become more conscious of this. My problem solving skills are minimal and I am not as confident as I need to be, but slowly I hope that I will improve. I am taking small steps because I know you're challenging me and thank you for that, thank you for giving me the tools and awareness to try and get me to believe in myself. My shadow has accumulated so much, so how do I truly forgive myself? How on this Earth can I do that? Thank you for the Angels, thank you Angels for your safety and guidance and protection. Please pass your loving kindness to all I know, have known and will know, pass it on to all I will never have the pleasure of knowing.

What do I want? What do I want? What do I want?

What do I want to share with the World? What do I have to offer to this World? Love, but how can I direct this Love? In what manner can I offer this Love that I have? I care about people. I care about human rights. Equality. Peace. I want to be authentic, to follow my heart, but it is still covered in some layers, some darkness, some thick stain. I Love Art and Music, and people being able to express themselves, to find an avenue for expression. To find a way to conquer the darkness, to express our Love without fear. I am not completely comfortable with the way that I express myself now. I feel like I am probably turning into myself but am definitely not there yet. The inside has to change before the outside can change I imagine. Thank you for giving me each breath, each moment and each day. Thank you for my Parents, my Family, my Friends, my Pets and thank you for all the people that have shared themselves with me over the years. Thank you for my job, thank you for the food I have to eat, thank you for the warmth of my unit and the luxuries that I have. Thank you for the strength of those around me, it has been amazing to see and be apart of. Thank you for Art and Music. Thank you for Love, thank you most of all for Love. Thank you for my shadow and the things I have learnt, thank you for the strength of body and mind to carry on. Thank you to all those who have worked with me and helped me learn what I have needed to learn. Thank you for the birds and all the animals I have eaten. Thank you for the things, people, situations I have or will ever forget to thank you for. Thank you for movies, and the actors and artists behind the work. Thank you for the people that sacrifice their time and money to help fellow human beings, please help me find the strength to conquer my fear. Thank you for the beach, the Sun, the Moon and again, Love. Amen.

Dear All,

I am here to purge my soul of the darkness that I have created. If I can change I know that one other person can change, which can impact the World greatly. I don't want to focus on the past but on this present moment and the appreciation I have for being alive. I know I want to help I just don't know how yet, Spirit will guide my way, I am sure of that.

Hear me now and know that the future is our right and our rights deserve to be acknowledged. Thank you for listening to me, I am grateful for each breath.

Amen.

Dear All,

Love will prevail. All your strength gives me strength and you all need to know that your power is available to you. If I believe you are all worthy of Love, then I myself must be worthy of Love. That just seems logical. This shame is deep, it penetrates the core of my being, I need help to expel it, to release it to the world. The water helps, oh the water helps.

I have begun a process of letting go. I cannot change the past, I literally have snippets of memories but no way of knowing what I have done. So I must trust my higher power in knowing that I tried my best with what I knew in each moment. I have to learn to feel that, to believe it, to know it within my heart. I must move on and move forward with the knowledge that I can help people, just like people can help me. I am eternally grateful for the beautiful human beings I have had the honour of already knowing, that have taught me so very many things.

The people of this World are strong, so strong. I have been apart of that as well. I must radiate Love at all times and share that with my fellow humans, animals and creatures. We are never alone, we have each other, we are apart of each other, we are connected. Self hatred is hating our history, hating our parents and the generations that have gone before. Goddess will guide me in the right direction. Thank you for all that is present in my life. You are all magical, your strength is phenomenal and breath taking, don't give up on yourself or the others around you. We are in this together.

Amen.

I pray that the light shines through me in times of need. I pray that the darkness does not envelope my soul again. I choose to let the past go and feel positive things for the future and trust that what I did was the best I could have done at the time. I literally knew no better, neither did the other human beings around me. These people I have known are powerful beyond measure, they have strength that brings confidence in me that the future can be saved.

I must try and stay aware for opportunities and ways to better respond to my environment.

I pray for the strength and guidance please and the wisdom to know things that I can and cannot change. I understand that great things are happening and the World is changing, I just wonder my place within it and how I can help.

I want to help. I do have Love in my heart, I do care, I guess the test is how much do I care and Love and how am I willing to show that?

Thank you for listening to me, my anxiety has dissipated.

May Light and Love prevail.

Thank you.

Amen.

The Sun is shining and it is a beautiful day and I am grateful for it, for the beauty can be overwhelming. Find within me Love. Love for myself and Love for fellow human beings. If I cannot Love myself, how can I Love another? If I find myself killing myself, I am killing my family and that is not what I want to do. I have made mistakes, but I want to make it better.

I have absolutely no idea what the future holds for me, only change, and I must embrace that or be left behind.

Please hear me God/Goddess,

This task is enormous, I am sure you have given it to me because I can handle it, with your grace and wisdom, but do I have the skills and strength to accomplish this task of self forgiveness? I want to, I want to so badly for Love. For Love is all that matters. It is the essence of who and what you are and what every human being I have met is. I know if I can change, anyone can change. I want to help people express themselves, find value in their stories of pain, shame and guilt. To find the light within the darkness. To turn something so painful into something beautiful, for there is something special we all have to share. My dream? Peace. Equality. Love prevails. Creativity. Expression. Joy. Laughter. Wonder. Awe.

Help me love myself, help me find that within me and I will share it with the World.

Thank you for listening to me.

Amen.

Dear Lord/Lady,

Please hear my cries. The sea she calls me but I cannot go. I cannot need her like I do. I want my heart from her floor but I am not deep enough yet. The uncharted depths, they call me, I hear her speak and I know she can hear me. I am angry with myself but I don't wish to hurt myself because I don't wish to hurt anyone else. We are all connected and I wish for Peace.

I know I have Love in my heart, somewhere underneath all the rubble of the wreckage of my past. I must learn to leave the wreckage of my past behind and take the treasures, for those memories are worth more than any gold or money in this World. Those treasures are the people I have met. The gifts of life that have been given to the World, each with their own dreams and fingerprint and qualities and strengths and weaknesses. They, the people are something to fight for. If I can unpack all the baggage I have held onto I know I will see all their faces clearly once again. I know I have Loved them. I know that, I have just lost touch with them. Thank you for the treasures of the people you have given to me. Thank you for their determination. Thank you for their strengths. Thank you for their smiles. They are amazing and I am the luckiest conduit of your grace to have received this gift of life.

Despite all the pain, the heart ache and loss I would do it all again to know, to believe that I have helped in some way.

I appreciate the time I have been given, you have given me so much and I couldn't ask for anymore. Just give me back my questions, I feel like I have lost my ability to ask questions. I like learning new things, I miss that. I have become stagnant in that dear Lord/Lady. A lot has been learnt here, more than I will ever comprehend.

I have found my heart, safe and secure at the bottom of the ocean, hidden away in a precious place and only the truth will set it free. My Love will be in its rightful place. The grace will have returned and we will be set free.

Now I have found my heart I must set it free and build a home within myself. A place of safety where flowers can bloom and love flows freely and clear like a river. A garden is where I would live, green grass, trees, flowers, river, rocks, birds, animals, somewhere like heaven. Blue skies, Sun. Stunning.

Thank you for giving me the gift of life. I am grateful for all that is and all that I am.

Where forgiveness is, Love is found.

Thats the truth.

Thank you kindly.

Amen.

Dear Goddess/God,

Thank you for the gift of my family and friends, for without them I would be nothing. I spent a lovely day with my Aunty, Uncle and Mother today and I am so happy that we are all alive and healthy to do such things. The fact we are all well enough and they took the time to spend some time with me was greatly appreciated. Being present was enough and their smiles were enough of a gift for me, so thank you graciously.

I will find a way to work through these issues and I appreciate all the friends I have and have had along the way, their generosity with their time and energy is immensely appreciated.

You have graciously given me enough time to walk a new and loving path, and while I know there will be difficult moments along the way, I will try my hardest to learn the lessons you want me to learn, without anger or resentment. I must find a pure happy place and ride the wave. I know that you only give me what I can handle at any one time and I appreciate what is happening to me. I want to feel that worthiness. I want others to feel that worthiness, because I know, if I am worthy, so are they, and that inner transformation will be hard, it will be painful but ultimately it will be worth it.

People deserve to smile and be happy, every one of us.
What do I stand for? Such a good question.
What are my values?
How do I move forward and evolve when I don't know my own value system?

The things I like the idea of are Integrity, Honesty, Expression (Communication), Team Work...

Thank you for a wonderful day, I appreciate everyone's time spent together today and for you listening to my ramblings on.

Amen.

Dear God/Goddess,

Here I stand, unaware and confused, feeling anxious and self indulgent. There is still anger in here, I can feel it, and I know not what I do. What is my purpose here dear Lord, I ask of you, what is my purpose?

I know you are testing me, and I know you only give me a certain amount of information as it is necessary to me, but here me now, I am lost and confused in this moment although I have found so much. I have had a good day with Brodie, and I have enjoyed my time with my family and friends, its just in this moment that I am not vibrating at my highest.

The absurdity of this place is making me think of things I probably shouldn't be thinking of.

I know I am being tested constantly, I just can't seem to make this work for me. What will I do Lord?

Thank you kindly for all that I have been given, the time of people that have strong hearts. Thank you for the Love.

Amen.

To All,

There must be a part of me that can look everyone in the eye. That is ultimately how we connect. I am vibrating at a high level of Love today and I wonder how many mistakes I have made? There is a part of me that knows that equality is possible, with all human beings. It was a split second moment where I couldn't look that woman in the eyes, but that was not from lust, I can't quite put my finger on what that was. I know there was a lesson there, and I am willing to learn it, I guess I need practice. How fascinating this must be. But I imagine if I was to help someone along the way my mission, whatever that may be, would be complete and I would be satisfied completely.

Thank you All for my Family, Friends, and everyone else in and of this World. I know we can find another way.

Pain and Love are universal, we just need to find a way for Love to shine through the darkness and that will take time, because everyone deserves to Love and be Loved, it is the greatest feeling in the World, nothing compares, not one word I have ever written compares to that feeling. Nothing I can create or do compares to that feeling and I am eternally blessed to have felt it in my lifetime. There are different kinds of Love and Caring but to find a person that you can connect with the way I did with Sarah, well I am eternally grateful.

I have much to learn here on this planet and you have given me the opportunity to meet the people that can teach me what I want to learn. These people I know and have met are my strength, their smiles and their gifts are something special, I do not have the words to express the feeling that I am feeling right now.

I don't know what my life has in store but I am ready to receive the guidance that will take me where I need to go. Thank you for my strengths and weaknesses and thank you for helping me learn how to be resilient. Please don't take me out into Space yet, I don't know enough about enough people to keep my mind from living in fear out there. That emptiness is vast but I know I can create memories to fill that void so my loneliness will no longer consume me. The darkness will not prevail, we will unite in Love and Light and the kingdom of Heaven will be within us all. Thank you.

Amen.

To All,

I feel frustrated at myself. I know I am trying my hardest here, I guess my expectations of myself are too high. I don't know what I think I should know before even learning it. I know mistakes give you the opportunity to learn, I guess I just need the bravery and resilience to face these mistakes. I know I have been protected and for that I am eternally grateful, I just want to repay the favour. I want to help the people around me, if they need help and I know taking care of myself is the best way forward. Change is the issue here. I have wanted everyone else to change without looking at myself and realising that its me that needs to change more than anyone. For me, if I don't find a way to change I don't know what I will do. I know I am somewhat doing the right thing, but needing approval constantly is tiring, to myself and to others. I was born all backwards and inside out and it does my head in on a daily basis, but I know I need to help myself otherwise I can't evolve. I want growth and change and empowerment and peace. I prey to you that I am trying my best here, so challenge me as you have been because I know if Divine Love is the price to pay for it, I will take it. I want that. I want to feel that Divine Beauty and Love, I want it for All of us. We have the means to find that within ourselves. Not one word, and as amazing as words are, there is not one word to describe the Love I have in my heart at this moment. I know there is more in there as well. By whatever means possible I must speak my truth, and I must listen to the truth of others.

The absurdity of this World is overwhelming at times, and in this moment I find it so.

Thank you for listening to my words and thoughts.

Thank you for my Family, Friends, Pets, Job, Home, Bed, Food, Water, Sanitation, Luxuries, Wealth, Abundance, Car, my able body, my senses, laughter, Love and Life.

Amen.

Dear God/Goddess,

I ask of you to help me become humble. Humble in my nature, words and actions. I wish to find within me the grace of your Spirit and the strength of being a servant to the people. Help me shed my layers of ego and let your Love shine through me. I ask for acceptance of my situation and forgiveness for past wrong doings. Being humble is important to me, for people are important to me. This World and its future is important to me and I wish to contribute to it positively please. I ask for your guidance and wisdom in carrying me to a place of humble light. I can promise that I will make mistakes along the way, I am sure of that, but if you help me with your power I can learn to forgive myself and evolve through the pain and turmoil. Being humble is your way, and your way is something I wish to attain, Divine Love. Thank you.

Amen.

To All,

I have been looking through photos and I cannot believe my eyes. I am in shock. What moments in my life, with amazing people. My memory has been tainted and I don't know where some of these wonderful memories are. My thoughts have tainted these moments. These people raised me and I love them all.

How does one become humble? My ego has been enormous and I have been arrogant beyond measure, that much I know. The pain gets in the way of making progress, and I don't want that. I want to make progress to move through this pain so I can show these people that I do care.

My past is a ship wreck, quite literally, but the treasures I have within my heart are priceless, jewels of the ocean. I just have to find my heart again, I know where I buried it, its time to dive deep into the depths and retrieve it to return the Love that has been given to me.

Thank you for my Family, Friends, Pets, Job, Car, Home, Food, Bed, Warmth, Choices, Rights.

Thank you for Life.

Amen.

Dear Goddess/God,

Thank you for giving me the light that I am feeling today. I have had an amazing day sharing it with people that I can see struggling. I feel like I am getting stronger at holding my intention in Love. I am happy that people have been looking into my eyes, connecting with me, although I know they are struggling. We are progressing through this, how beautiful this is. Thank you for giving me the ideas that you have today, I am eternally grateful for all the darkness and all the light. I wouldn't go back in time and change one thing, because I know, moving forward I can offer light and Love to people and see their hearts change. That is something phenomenal. I know my defences were down today, but I fought my way through it and I can feel myself getting stronger and stronger. I have ideas again, and they are wonderful ideas, ideas that can change things, ideas that have purpose and meaning, that have value, ideas that could change the World in which we all occupy.

Free Health Care. Care being the operative word here, because that's where Love lies.

A goal greater than loving one other individual, a goal to share my Love with the World and all its inhabitants. Power and control have condemned us to the horrors that the World has been, but it is changing and it will change some more. With every individual effort there is progress. With self-love and self-care we can pass that down to our Children.

I want to learn as much as I can about as many people as I can, so please help me with my memory and minds ability to retain information.

I want to offer my acceptance of my part in this World. I have no idea the depth or measure of the part but I will play my role wholeheartedly. I accept your guidance and wisdom, knowing that your Divine Love will guide me to a place where the suffering will end.

I ask of you to help dissolve my jealousy and the hurt and anger it involves. Guide me with acceptance, wisdom and Love.

Feeling secure within oneself, what a wonderful idea, I wonder how one attains such a thing. I imagine being able to rely on oneself.

I want people that find themselves dealing with feelings of attraction towards children to be able to talk about it, because there has to be a solution to this problem without someone offending or killing themselves and I want to help. Every life is worth living, we all have barriers but I know that we can find a solution. People need to find a way to talk about these worries without judgement because fear would be a total barrier to divulging this kind of information and shame, the shame is immense. Acceptance and commitment therapy would probably help, just by the sound of the name it sounds like a great idea. Thank you for listening to my words and ideas, I am eternally grateful for all the Love I have received. It is my turn to return it and dedicate it to all those people I love immensely. I dedicate my work to everyone else, we are all in this together and I now find myself in and of this World with purpose and meaning, so I can move forward and learn and Love.

Amen.

Dear Goddess/God,

I am trying to hold the vision and I think I am doing quite well. Obviously it will take a lot more practice but I am getting there. I can hear you more clearly now so I am finding the challenges at a level I can handle. Thank you for all the kind people that I am surrounded with who are teaching me things that I need to know to progress. My heart aches for freedom. My heart aches for Love. My heart beats Love, pure Love but my mind is in a place where danger lurks and darkness knows my name. My demons have demons and I know they know each other too well. My heart has been buried at the bottom of the ocean and I need to retrieve it please, so please help me do that. I know we will find things that have yet to be found but thats the adventure right there. I know I must trust the process more and not wish or hope for anything, but dream of goals that I could achieve and possibilities that could come true.

I want to have a party on an island somewhere, with Family and Friends, in the Sun having fun and relaxing and enjoying each other, food, mocktails and the water. I want that. Is that something I shouldn't dream of? I want to enjoy people and my space and find myself. I want to know who I am and why I am here. I truly don't wish to possess anyone, especially those I care about. I have had enough of that. I don't want to suffer either, suffer because I cannot get my way or because of jealousy and instability within myself. I want to be able to stand strong and have conviction, I don't want to be indecisive all the time, I want to do things I enjoy and remember them. I want to study and share myself with the World while others share themselves with me. I want to care and be cared for but know that I am my strength. That I am capable and ready to take a challenge on without fear of failure. Knowing the failure is a learning opportunity and something essential to growth.

I have to start believing that I can achieve the goals I put in place if I try, as simple as that. If I try.

I have made many attempts at study and have walked away feeling discouraged and weak, but I am not going to give up because education is essential to growth of an individual. Life is also education but also structured education would be surely handy in a World of todays structure. What are the rules anyway? There are some that can't be broken and there are some that should for the good of evolution. We can't stand still any longer and I must take that first step, I must move with the people and learn to evolve. We will walk in unity one day and I hope I get to see life for a long time to come. I always thought that there would be never enough time to see or know or experience all the things that this World and these people have to offer, but I know if I take it slow and value the time I have and spend it wisely I will learn all I need to know. I want to study social work and I got a sign today that I should so I am going to trust the universe and take that opportunity to research Holmesglen Institute. Thank you for the choices that I have today because madness nearly ended my life and I am eternally grateful that I am alive today. I appreciate the small amounts of information you are trickling into my consciousness to bring me into whatever reality this is, for you have given me a great enough reason to bear any how. I will live by the quote 'you can bear any how if there is a big enough why', and I thank Dr. Frankl for that because that came from enduring great hardship but it will help me immensely. Love is the big enough why, Love. ♥Amen.

Dear Goddess/God,

I am here and I exist and I am eternally grateful for this fact. Thank you for the life you have given me and the blessings I have received. I do not know what you have in store for me but I am trying to take up your challenges with an open heart. I must learn to forgive myself but I think that will come in time when I feel I have achieved something. Although I know I have made some improvements lately so I am proud of them and acknowledge that great things begin with small steps. I do feel myself becoming stronger with each test and I know that I am only given what I can handle. Or at least thats what I believe, so I am sticking to that. This World is absurd, totally and utterly absurd and needs to be explored with no fear. I am trying to look people in the eyes until they look away first, I have no idea what it achieves but I believe it to be a sacred challenge, so here we go. I do not have the words to describe the sensations and feelings within my body right at this moment. How does one express such wonder and awe, such profound Love? I imagine with actions. I can only work through these challenging emotions and states of mind and evolve through them. Thank you for listening to my ramblings.

Amen.

Dear Goddess/God,

My faith is becoming stronger and my ability to withstand some criticism is gaining momentum. I am guessing that my resilience is building somehow, through facing my fears and challenging myself everyday. I don't ever want to pass on the feeling of inadequacy that I felt today when I made a mistake and saw the face that my co-worker pulled. I know its a test and he was not disrespecting me as a person but that look literally sent me to tears. I cried ever so slightly and I would hate for any child, or any human being to feel like that in their life, but although it was challenging I managed the wave and I got through it. I now see it as an essential lesson to be learnt. Actually if I am honest, I am enjoying the failures because they seem to hold for me the greatest insights. The joy is rewarding and my fear responses are diminishing very much. I did sweat today when I realised I had made a mistake, but I admitted that I had probably done more pallets in that area than I had first thought. I became more aware after that. My ability to drive the machine will improve I just must realise that I am learning and not to anger easily, for that helps no one. I guess that anger comes down to feeling inadequate for the task, as if I can't do it and that goes deeper into an attack on my whole self, instead of seeing it as a momentary lapse in my ability to complete a task due to fear responses.

I was thinking about the importance of forgiveness, most importantly self-forgiveness. Which is something that I must work on, but my thoughts today focused on the actual feeling of guilt slowly diminishing. That tight feeling that feels like its eating your internal organs and your cells. Maybe with meditation, focused energy on others higher selves, helping each other in times of need, nourishing each other with Love, giving food and time to people we care about, we will have less guilt, less hate for ourselves and others. Because we hate ourselves which means we hate each other and that is going to destroy us, it will annihilate us where we stand or sit. Judging ourselves is simply judging another, thats comparison right there. How can one person be beautiful without another being ugly to have that comparison. And how can we have sub-groups of human beings? How can we have Human Rights but have sub-groups with human rights separated into these groups? It makes absolutely no sense to me. We are all human beings, there should be no divisions, barriers between us all reaching our full potential, our full creative potentials.

I keep Dr Frankl's quote strong within my mind and heart that "if there is a great enough why you will bear any how", and those are not my words but I find my truth in it and I will live by it. It feels as if it gives my life purpose and meaning.

I am now on an onwards journey towards the depths of knowing who I am and who I can become. The past is in the past, I am sure I can visit it but I don't have to live there, I will gain insight and wisdom from the experiences that I have had but the future is what I am looking forward to. I have much to learn, and much to give so here I go!

Thank you for all your guidance, through the wisdom of other people. Thank you for the love and sharing, I will not refuse peoples offer of sharing anymore. Thank you for life itself, I am blessed everyday to wake up and experience this amazing place.

Amen.

Dear God/Goddess,

I have found this garden and it is beyond beautiful, magical and it radiates light. Thank you for letting me enter. I know I am far from perfect to accept constant vision of this garden but I will try my best to do what I can to get into it more often. It wakes me up and brightens my day and ideas, the clarity of consciousness is phenomenal. I have much to learn of this planet but I am excited for my future prospects. There is a mote, a place to bathe outside this castle, it would be refreshing I imagine. Inside the grounds of the castle, the outside in particular, the garden is centre and it shines, radiates even. It is tranquil, peaceful beyond anything I have ever known, nothing can compare to this place, nothing would come close. There are trees, birds, ferns, grass, soil, trees, water, and I have a hammock because that would be absolutely comfortable. There would be the warm Sun shining down on me in the day and the Moon and the Stars at night, no pollution, a blanket of Stars. I would be comfortable enough to be naked, the breeze would caress my skin and keep me cool. I would wander around talking to the animals and the creatures of the land. It would sound peaceful, birds chirping, talking to one another, communicating small but wondrous things.

I have found my heart. I have reclaimed it, it is now mine. No one can own it any longer, it is my choice to give Love freely and selflessly. I can repair it and take good care of it. I must become as authentic as possible, following my heart and learning everything that I can to take back to this garden and let it grow.

I want to throw a party. I want it to be big and fun and amazing. I want my family and friends there and others, I don't know who yet, but I am sure it would be amazing.

Boundaries and the ability to say "No", I must learn this. I don't want to be a follower, I want to be a leader, but what does that entail, how does one lead? And in what situation does one lead? Boundaries, I would want my children to learn them so why shouldn't I know what they are. They are profoundly important for the safety of an individual.

Thank you for this coffee, it's amazing!

Amen.

Dear Goddess/God,

I feel a pang of anxiety within my body, I cannot locate its source but it is surely there. It could be from watching a movie about a Nun and the Devil, but all I know is that I won't be driven crazy. I have already made one vow in my life and that was dedicating my willingness to participate in this life wholeheartedly for the goal of helping people, so that is what I will do. I will make another vow, but it may be like the first, to serve you, Spirit to the best of my ability. I make a promise to you today to take my medication religiously for the rest of my life, I haven't complied with my medication before but I agree that it is helping me and I need that help. I will stop any medication that stops me from having children, so that is just something I would like to do, or any medication that may harm my baby. I would resume said medication after it was safe to do so, so that is my promise to you. I know I have needed help for many years now, and I have tried over and over again, so I hope my efforts have pleased you enough. I know I have tried my best with the tools I had along the way.

I will take a journey around this country first, then around the world to help try and forgive myself, because thats where the healing begins. I know I can do this and although there is fear, I know I can overcome it.

Thank you for your guidance, I know this mission is important, all I can do is be brave and believe that Love is enough, and that Love can conquer all dark forces. I know it will take time, because change is hard and its painful but the rewards are golden, priceless and courage is within us all to fight for our birthrights. Peace, Joy, Love, Health, Happiness.

Amen.

Dear Goddess/God,

Give me the strength to speak out against injustice and fight for equality because women's rights, or lack there of have been hijacked and taken for granted for too long now. I am angry and in pain here, this is not right and I have apologised for my existence for long enough. Something must be done. We are all human beings and we have birthrights and its time for us women to claim ours, and when we are brave enough to do the same, we'll then join in equality. There will be change, that much I can feel, that much I know. We absolutely, with no shadow of a doubt have the capabilities to rise from the ashes and claim our birthrights, and that is nothing to be ashamed of. I don't quite know yet how this will be done, I know there are women on the ground now working these things out. I will not judge, for I am past that, I have judged people for too long now and I have been judged in return, I must be brave now and speak, raise my voice so others can hear me, just like I am hearing them. Thats all I need to do. I had to learn so many things and I wouldn't take back any of it, not one experience, never, not for what I have gained and what I have to offer. I have much to learn and much to offer. We all have value and that must mean me too, so that is a nice feeling.

We will rise against injustice and tell our stories, our tears and pain will never define us, we are not victims, we are survivors, there will be victory!

Thank you for the insights, thank you to All who have shared themselves with me, we will be safe, we will find that Love within and be reunited with our hearts and claim our birthrights.

Amen.

Dear God/Goddess,

Thank you for hearing me today. My grief is palpable and very present within me today. I have reached a point of no return and I must endure this pain for the victory of Love. There is so much beauty surrounding me but I still find myself in tears, and that's what grief feels like. I know there is a lesson to be learnt here and I am determined to learn it I just need to express this pain before it consumes me. I will let go of them. I must to help myself, them and the World. I cannot walk around with this pain in my heart any longer, not when life is so beautiful and there is strength and kindness to be created and felt. I will cry until the tears dry up and all I can do is smile. Because I long to bring happiness into the World.

I know not where this journey will take me, I just know that I must be brave and fight for my rights to be the role model I would want my children to see. I am ready for this. Bring It!

I am eternally grateful for these experiences God/Goddess, I have learnt so much, I want Light and Love in my Life so I can share that with people. Thats all I have left now, Love.

Amen.

Dear God/Goddess,

I didn't even know I had rights, I don't even believe I thought I was a human being at some point in time. I didn't know that these rights are given to you at birth, they are our birth rights and they have been stripped from us. I know they can make us strong if we believe we are worthy of them. I must get past the intellectual part of it and really feel that I am worthy, within my soul, deep within me. To know that my existence is worthy of being lived. I had no idea these gifts were bestowed upon me, and I am just coming to the realisation now. But these rights, these ideals about equality are strength and life giving. They fill me with a hope that some day I will become one person, whole again, commune with my soul, live in that garden peacefully with no guilt or shame. To be pure of heart and mind and body, to have Love in every cell. I see so much Love and layers of history, its fascinating and glorious to watch on a daily basis. The World is full of peoples ideas, their thought forms, their genius, their Love.

Not only is there humans' Love there is Spirit's Love everywhere. The Sea and the Sun, the Moon and the Earth, and us, we, the glory of Love.

The path to self forgiveness is to let the guilt dissipate slowly, until it has reached a point of no control, where it still exists but the control it has is nothing in comparison to what it was. And the shame, oh the shame, that too needs to dissipate in time and with good deeds and self compassion. For I am determined to find my way back to my soul and God/Goddess. I know Love is pure and I know it is possible to feel that, and we all deserve it, each and every one of us. I ask for Love to be given and received, in great proportions, even to those who believe they don't deserve it. For every problem there is a solution, we just have to be brave enough to walk the path to find it. For those paths have yet to be walked, because we are where we are for a reason. I don't know who I am yet, there is much to learn, but I ask of my higher powers to help guide me, and help me find a way to go on a holiday. Thank you kindly.

Amen.

Good Morning Goddess/God,

I am feeling rather strange but I am alive so I am happy about that. The Sun is shining and I will allow myself one coffee this morning. I don't know what has triggered this uncomfortable feeling but it is covering me and making me feel unclean and uncomfortable.

I feel like I have been on the Titanic and everyone else has died, and I am still in the water and waiting for someone to save me. But I didn't realise I had to save myself. So I will. I will journey into Outback Australia and lose myself and let go of all that has held me under water for so long. I have my heart, I found it at the bottom of the ocean, at the Marianna Trench, I have her, I just need to swim to shore and do something with my life before I die. My stories so far are the stories of others and I cannot tell them like they need to be told. I literally don't know where I have been, that is a secret between Spirit and the stars, I guess I have to find myself somewhere far away from where I am now. I must take with me trust, faith, appreciation and grace. I must walk and stand strong and face my fears like I have done here.

My mind is so jumbled and I feel like I am drowning. I know I know how to swim but maybe I just need to relax a little and let go. My grip is so tight and I don't want to let go. I know I can but I guess I am afraid, of what, I am truly unsure of in this moment. These moments have defined me, I have built a story around these experiences and I cannot see whats ahead of me, I am guessing thats where trust and faith need to come into it. After all the messages you would think I would learn, so I will. I must believe. What does that energy look or feel like to you Nicole? This synergy.

Thank you for the depths and the wonder but most of all, The Love.

Amen.

Dear Lord,

Please hear my prayer, I have sinned and my heart is hurting. I have much to learn but the criticism in my own mind is deafening. My shadow looms large while the light fades. I prey for forgiveness, the ability to move forward, to move on, to create something much larger than myself. Please hear me Lord. I am grateful for the stories, the sharing of others lives and wisdom, I just must move past this idea of not actually knowing, this concrete idea of never knowing anything for sure, help release me from this curse and I will walk with faith in each step. I know that to know is something of an absurd concept and it would ruin everything, and you have given me free will and two paths to walk down. I choose your path. I will have to rebuild myself, find a way back to your graces, your place of highest, pure white Love.

I ask my Angels and Goddess/God to help me see the light, the truth, help me share it. It is my choice now, my noble choice.

This is my life, this journey is mine and mine alone and I cannot and will not let you down. I know of nothing else, I only know what you allow me to know and that I am sure is quite little in comparison to what there is to know about this universe. I am almost angry and in pain today but I have laughed and smiled and learnt great things, so thank you to Paula for sharing herself with me, greatly appreciated.

I want no more judgements for I have judged enough, and I must stop. For any judgement I make upon another or myself, well it works both ways.

I haven't done what has been in my heart for a long time. My friends, oh my dear Lord, my friends. The ache.

I did the best I could with what I knew at the time. I must internalise that and live it, to know it, feel it, breathe it deep within.

Thank you for this apple I am eating, it is crisp and juicy and I am thoroughly enjoying it. I thank you for my clean clothes, a warm shower, the toilet, the roof over my head, food, choices and the ability to dream. Thank you for the insight and the good memories.

Bless everyone, family, friends, work colleagues, people I make eye contact with, all human beings and all animals, my two cats and myself. Thank you kindly.

Amen.

Dear God/Goddess,

I am here to profess that all my heart has ever wanted is to Love and be Loved, but I never knew how to do this enormous task, because it was and is important to me that I do it right. This is no easy task, this requires a lot of preparation and dedication and research and time. I am ready to free myself from who I was and be the new me. I will forgive in time, that is a process, but I want to let go of her completely. I have more Love to give to humanity that I am able to share at this moment, but I want to release her and be released. I ask my Angels and both your guidance and assistance in helping me make this happen, I know it is getting to the right time. I am not asking for Love to come into my life now, I am asking to release this woman into the World where she belongs, to her family, not in my heart and mind any more. I am eternally grateful for the Love we shared but I haven't grown, I have stayed stagnant and cold. I want more than that please, I want to feel that grand Love. Divine Love is eternal and grand by design but the Love of a family would be priceless in this lifetime and I want that. I am working hard to fulfil all my needs, for only I can. I wish to impart on my children and the World values that give strength. I want children to feel their own worth and value, to feel these things within their bodies, in their hearts, for their minds may try and fight them but we will have given them the resources to know when their heart is talking to them. I have to learn that I have birthrights, for to become aware of this fact will give me power, the kind of power to manifest great things. I will build an empire from the ground up with a solid foundation and it will be beautiful to see, just like us all.

I thank my Angels and Spirit for giving me the new perspective on these uncomfortable and uneasy feelings, for these lessons are priceless and necessary to be shared. I thank you for the job I have, the food I eat, my car, choices, free will, Love, connection, sanitation, a warm bed and all the people I have had the honour of meeting throughout my life.

Help me with this task ahead of me please, help me release this Love back to where it came from, return it to her with eternal gratitude. Help me focus on my new goals and give me the strength to achieve the things

I need to achieve. I refuse to die from a broken heart when I have been shown so much Love. I must, absolutely must return the Love that has been given to me. Help me attain this goal. I ask of you nothing more.

Amen.

Good Morning Goddess/God,

I am finding that my existence is finding meaning and purpose and that is an amazing feeling. I still have mornings where getting out of that comfortable bed is hard, but it is greatly worth it. I am developing new strategies to deal with old issues and implementing them slowly over time, which feels amazing. I know they will turn into new habits, healthy ways of living that I can model to my children when I am blessed to have them one day. I am finding my perspective changing in the way I am dealing with the set backs that I have and the way in which I deal with problems that arise. I am guessing that my resilience is building which feels amazing. I am clearing out my past, and illuminating my shadow parts, and finding lessons and gold where there was once pain. I am trying to fulfil my needs when they arise, for no one should have to try and fill them for me, I will become the master of that. I am trying to smile a lot more, but I must say it feels foreign and strange, although my heart is singing my face doesn't match whats happening on the inside, very strange. I am trying though, as they say, fake it until you make it I guess. The insights have been fascinating to experience, I am eternally grateful for everything that I am experiencing. I am beginning to get more faith in my ability to handle and process all this information, this journey is fascinating and wondrous and the people I am meeting, well thank you for that dear Spirit. I am retaining more information which is so exciting because it means something to me, people's names and learning about their stories, their families, their history, I love it. I appreciate all the time I have to myself and I appreciate all the time I am spending with other people. Both time well spent. Nature is powerful, she can heal us all.

It is World Peace Day today, and I am wondering what I can do to contribute to this day in a positive way? I know I can take care of myself, listen to myself and take action in caring for my body, mind, spirit. For if I am to care for anyone else in this World, I must learn to care, to truly care for myself. How could I find value in someone else if I don't find value in myself. I don't want to live in my comfort zone anymore. I have learnt a lot. On World Peace day I will try and smile more. Live more congruent with my values. I will not compare myself to any other human being, because I am not them and they are not me. Our experiences are different but we can share Love. That is universal, something unshakeable when it is cultivated and valued within the self. When we find it it can be nourished, it can transmute pain into passion and Love. We all belong here, no matter who you are, I believe that whole heartedly. On World Peace Day I want to express my Love and Caring for every human soul that has ever existed, will ever exist and to the higher powers giving us this blessing that is Life. I know there are deeply engrained issues and such fragile pain that exists, but I know that Love can heal these things. The shame and the guilt does not need to be the only thing that exists in this World, there is more, I know that. I don't know much but I know these things for sure, I have felt them within my body, they exist in a place that is beyond words, beyond my ability to express them, I just know because I have felt them.

On World Peace Day I want to look into the eyes of others and share connection, even if only for a moment, to share a moment of Love that is eternal, that means something. I know there are a few days that are associated with this movement so I will live by Mahatma Gandhi's words and "be the change I want to see in the World". It starts with me, as an individual, as one human being wanting a better place for myself and the people I care about. If I can be brave and look darkness in the face and stand there rooted in Love I can make this moment magical. I can learn and proceed, I can evolve and imagine. I can Live and Love.

World Peace Day is something I can try and create everyday, there doesn't need to be one assigned day a year for this to be thought about, I need to think about how I can implement these things everyday of my life, from moment to moment, with awareness and passion and enthusiasm. I see the spark of life force and Love in every human being, no matter their history. I know there is a solution to every problem, we just have to be brave enough to start talking about the real issues. We need to face the shame and guilt and pain with courage and determination because we are all worth it. We have value, beyond what we see, we are multidimensional beings with offerings that transcend everyday existence. We are Love and Light, we are more than we have been, more than we think we can be and more than anyone has made us feel.

I need to make myself realise my potential, and I will, slowly, in time, because time is what I have and I must spend it wisely.

I want to study and help people help themselves. I want to see people achieve their goals. There is nothing in the World more satisfying than seeing the smile on someones face when they have a realisation that they can accomplish something they never thought they could. I will work hard to do that, because I know I am inclusive of that. I want to know that I am capable and that I can accomplish things I set out to do, because I can and I have.

On another note, my heart doesn't cry out for anyone anymore, my heart isn't broken, she is mending well thank you kindly. I refuse to die from a broken heart when I have been shown so much Love and strength in my life from amazing beautiful people. I will not let that go to waste, if I focus on the heartache of losing these people I will not recall the Love and good times that we shared and that is what I will keep in my heart. I will not let this ruin me, ever. As Shakespeare said, "It is better to have loved and lost than to never have loved at all". And I won't give up, because I have time to Love more people, there are many people in this World to Love, I have enough for many more to come.

Thank you for the people within my heart and life and everyone I will ever meet and connect with. Thank you for the gifts of life and my life.

Amen.

Good Morning Goddess/God,

I will purge my soul then I will write a poem about humanity. I am feeling very loving today, my energy is high. I want to be a good role model this is the truth, so to do that I must feel empowered by my choices, and grounded in knowing the reason for the choice I have made. It is not my place to understand why others Love what they do Love and why they cannot stop, it is my place to walk a new path, to use parts of my brain that I have yet to use. To create not follow. This journey is not meant to be easy. My reasons for choosing my choices are essential to my growth and empowerment, and thats what I want, to be a strong confident woman that is grounded within herself and her beliefs. I am beginning to feel and believe that I have ideas to offer this World, and that feels amazing. I am absolutely loving talking to other human beings and finding out about them and their families, I can see such strength in these people. Flames. Power. I see beauty within them all, I see their souls shining through. This vision is celestial and Divine and I am blessed to be a conduit of this Love. These tiny droplets of water that make up the ocean are us, we are the ocean and everything that lives within it. We are the sea and the stars and the clouds and the birds. We are creation, everything in between, what came before and what can last eternity.

What we can do is surrender, surrender the shame, the guilt. We can find Love. This World is forgiving and there is help for all.

Sea Breeze

Etherial waves contemplating time
Our essence deeply shadowed
Light is our unity

I have come to the conclusion that I can do this, each challenge is a lesson and I must remember that. Thank you for your guidance. I have enjoyed every last coffee I have consumed and I will walk the path that no one else has walked, for that is what evolution is.

Thank you for my last coffee, the car I sit in, sanitation and water, food, choices, joy, Love, bike riding, basketball, people, friends, family, pets and animals. Thank you for the sea and music, movies, sport, progress. Thank you for beauty and the theatre, the rain, babies and children, for teenagers and adults, for human beings in general. Thank you for art and creative expression. Thank you for life and the gifts I have received over time.

Amen.

Good Morning All,

I am feeling amazing today, it was hard to wake up but when I am awake I am in Love with the World. I have so many thoughts and ideas running through my brain I feel a little overwhelmed as to where to begin. Maybe its just how high I am vibrating then, because my energy is big today. I don't feel like I am being lazy, I am living in line with my values more and more, I am feeling like I can support myself through the hard times. I want to become self sufficient, I want to be able to totally rely on myself. I had to ask my Mum for a loan for the car the other day for the brakes but if I hadn't of asked her I wouldn't have been able to get them done. So I need to save money. I want to be a good Mother, but way before having children I must learn to model good and value driven behaviour. So I must learn to care for myself, learn my own value and what I am worth, because these are the gifts that will be precious to pass on to my children. I must also learn how to stick up for my rights, boundaries, to say no, to be assertive. Face challenges with a positive attitude and to try, to simply try. I am not scared anymore. I don't feel scared. I am content being alone with myself, it no longer causes distress. I have walked out of that cage I had made my home for so long and I have rolled down that grassy hill into a patch of bright yellow flowers. The Sun is shining and I can feel the breeze. My thoughts are wild today and the Sun is shining bright. People are everywhere and I am ready for whats to come.

Thank you kindly.

Amen.

Good Morning God/Goddess,

I want to live. I am happy. I am content and I have things to achieve. I feel like there are things I can contribute to my community and my country. I know not what these things are yet but I am truly excited to find out what they are. I cannot recall why I wanted to die that day, or any other day that I felt that way, but I must say that I am eternally grateful that I didn't die. That I survived. That there were people there to help me. I do not know what will come but it can only be beautiful, I can feel that. I have nothing but Love left to give, I am giving away my ego, I am surrendering it. It has and is being dissolved. I have accepted to the best of my ability my situation. So I ask of my Angels and the Goddess/God to please accept my vow of acceptance for the journey ahead. My need to know has been an issue for me, but it seems illogical now. I want this journey to continue and for my growth to flourish and bring light to the World. My dreams will come true, in time I believe that. I am dedicated to working on them with all my capacity to do so. I am eternally grateful for this life I have been given, for the people I have met and the Love I have been shown. I am eternally grateful for my choices and Divine Guidance and Love. I will return the Love I have been shown, I can promise that much.

Thy will be done.

Amen.

Dear God/Goddess,

I find myself with an issue at work. There is a work colleague that is out spoken about topics that are playing on my mind and I have noticed a few missed opportunities to say something. I know I am being tested and writing about it won't necessarily work the situation out but I am becoming increasingly frustrated. I guess I don't really like confrontation and it is a male work colleague but that is no excuse to be honest. These issues that he is bringing up in me are important and I haven't found my voice. I want to stand strong and be a strong woman so I am asking for more awareness I guess, or a quicker response time to this persons attitude. I have noticed that I am heading toward judging him because I am getting frustrated with myself for not saying something. I don't want to judge him or myself and I don't want to get angry. I need to work on the absence of rights I have felt like in my lifetime. I cannot stand up for my rights or self if I didn't know I had rights and that I am worthy of these innate rights in the first place.

I am worthy of these rights because I try every day to spread kindness and a sense of caring. I am worthy of these rights because I care about people and want to see their happiness prevail. I am worthy of these rights because I believe in love, and I am loveable like all human beings are. No amount of people telling me they Love me will ever satisfy my need to feel Loved by my own self. I couldn't believe anyone else Loving me if I don't believe that I can Love myself.

I must learn to take small bites out of life, because I expect a lot from myself. My expectations of myself are incredibly high, I must learn to appreciate the small steps I am taking and the strengths that I have.

I can feel the depth of this place, sometimes that feeling can become overwhelming, not necessarily bad overwhelming but overwhelming all the same. There is so much to learn and I am trying too hard to rush this beautiful process. Slow down Nicole, please, slow down.

I feel the need to find my voice. I don't know where it is but I must find it. I know there is a higher mission here for me, but Love is what kept me here.

Spirit Loves me, like All of Us, so I must find that Love within myself, to feel it, to know it, despite all other things, that spark, that essence that is only mine, that was given to me at birth, at conception, Love.

Thy will be done.

Amen.

Dear God/Goddess,

I see now there is no one here to blame. This situation is bigger than myself and I wish not for suffering to continue. I wish for freedom and strength to unite us, mixed in with Love and happiness. I feel lighter in this moment, I feel like I can breathe again. I know that forgiveness is a process but I am sure I have found the reason to forgive myself, that no one is to blame, for none of us knew any better. I will fight my hardest to make sure that no souls get left behind. No one is less important here, not one soul. Mistakes have been made but they are there to teach us great things. The shame and the guilt will fade away with time, that much I am sure. My values will shine brighter as I learn to value myself and create the person I am inside, in my heart. With no forgiveness comes judgement and I truly wish not to judge, not myself or another human being. Judgement does not align with my values, it divides us and creates unhealthy ways of thinking. I must reconcile blame, that one stings, blame is a poison, I imagine personal responsibility would help with that. I made the choices I have made so I will live with the consequences. There is pain left from these choices I have made but that pain can be experienced and moved through, freeing yourself for more pleasurable experiences.

There is limitless potential for the human spirit. There are ways to experience this World not defined yet, unexplored, there are other places to go and stories to be told. I wonder, I really wonder where we could go with all this Love.

I have no other words tonight, thank you kindly.

Thy will be done.

Amen.

Good evening God/Goddess,

I am exisiting within a realm of contemplation tonight. I surrender all to you both and to the Angels, I surrender all guilt, shame, anger and negative feelings. I wish to release myself of these emotions for they do not serve my higher purpose and I want forgiveness. I want forgiveness to heal me, make me shine brighter and give light out into the world. I want acceptance of thoughts and feelings without judgements, I want my mistakes to bring me wisdom and I want the pain to bring me power. The grief is going I can feel that, I am feeling lighter but still congested and tired. I must remember I have been mentally ill for many years and that recovery is possible, so I must give myself the time to heal. I am working my way through stages and phases and whatever else I need to, but I am determined to come to a state of forgiveness. I want that more than anything. Because I only knew what I knew at the time, I was unaware values even existed so how was I supposed to make a choice like that.

I am developing values now and that feels amazing. I will forgive myself because then we can all forgive ourselves and move forward towards Love where we all belong.

Thy will be done.

Amen.

Dear God/Goddess,

I have been unwell and overwhelmed. I have rested and slept and travelled to far away places in my dreams. I have been learning a lot as always and appreciate the wisdom and grace you have bestowed upon me. I am in the process of self forgiveness here and I want it more than anything at this point in my life. I also want to let her go, so with guidance and wisdom I ask that you help release from me my need to hold on to these things that are not serving me. The pain is being reconciled and I am getting stronger. I am literally experiencing growing pains within my body, its so strange. I ask for help with releasing these forces that are no longer serving me, moments of pain. I want to release them from my cells and my heart and mind. I am finding my place in this World and I am finding ways to enjoy and find Love. I am taking care of myself more and listening to my body, heart and soul. Because I know all I can do is my best like everyone else and we will all get to where we are going. I am finding great purpose in becoming a Social Worker, I truly feel like it is what I am meant to be doing with my life. I feel like my values and goals are aligned with its mission. I am beginning to find worth in myself greater than money and that I can provide for myself wholeheartedly. I am finding out that I am actually capable and I can achieve things I set out to do, and I am eternally blessed by Spirit with these gifts for me to share with the World.

With this I leave you with a small prayer about letting go of the past, self forgiveness and Love.

Please hear me Goddess/God,

Although I have fallen I will rise again knowing that you will guide me from my mistakes with Love and Kindness.

I am ready to let go of what has been,
While taking with me the lessons for what will be,

I have reconciled the pain of the past enough to know that forgiveness is the ultimate way for me,

I shall walk that path from this day forward with Love and Understanding.

Love is our unity,
Love is Peace.

Thy will be done.

Amen.

Dear All,

I feel as if I have woken from my coma, thank God/Goddess. I am alive and breathing, with a little help from Sia, so thanks. I made it out alive and I can stand in the darkness, there is no darkness too dark for me now, all lights are too bright for me at the moment, too much stimulation. I have had a few realisations in the car as well.

1. I must learn to cultivate and practice compassion and loving kindness towards myself and others, it is essential to my growth and happiness. Learn more on these subjects at a later date.

2. In wanting to let the past go I couldn't quite work out why I couldn't let myself leave high school and all my friends behind, but I now realise that I was probably the most authentic around those people than I have been in a long time. I shared love with those people, I loved them and they loved me in return, and I wanted that feeling back, I wanted those moments back and I can't have them back, too much has happened to me since then, I have gathered too many experiences to integrate that it will take time to become authentic and whole but I know that I can take away the Love I have for those people I shared High School with, the memories, the laughs and kindness. I am completely ready to leave that behind and move forward because thats what is already happening, I can feel that, I know that within my heart and soul, and if I am meant to see anyone of those people again I know I will see them and nothing will change that. I haven't processed a lot of things, and it is starting to happen for me and I am sure it will continue to happen, I just know that I am ready to move forward and I am ready to live my life.

Life is so much like driving a car I swear, and especially at night because your headlights only light up some of the road and if you focus on the part of the road you cannot see it can be scary, but if you focus on the parts that are lit up for now and trust that the light will guide you through the darkness, you will get there safely. And I guess your choice of speed can influence how scary the ride can be and those choices you have are what would be called free will I imagine, because although you think you're in control of this vehicle thats not entirely the truth, there are so many other extraneous variables that come into play that I am not sure where to even start to think what or who is in control. There is most definitely a higher power in control, and if there wasn't what would life be like, what would driving on the road by yourself be like? I am losing track of my ability to express myself coherently. All I know is that those feelings that have just passed through me have been worth every moment of it. There was a philosophical question that goes something like this, "in your darkest, most depressed, loneliest moment would you do it all again?" Or something like that, it is a lot more eloquent and makes sense, but as Dr. Frankl says, "if there is a big enough reason you will bear almost any how", well yes I do believe Love is that reason and I can answer that question now as a hands down yes I would do it all again. I have been thinking about that. But if I had of found a way to destroy my soul would I have? If I had of sourced that information, prepared for that end would I have ended my souls journey? I don't know what that would of meant for existence if we are all connected and such. I do remember having thoughts though of people, and if there was anyone that cared I wouldn't have wanted to hurt them by killing myself, because I don't want to hurt people, I don't have that desire within me and that thought hurts my heart. Anyway, so I have taken more steps towards helping myself I think than towards killing myself. I always knew that I needed help, from a young age I knew that I needed to keep trying to get help, and I have been guided and shown the way by many and I am eternally grateful for that and their help. I know that there is no one on this planet that I wouldn't care about, for no reason would there be that I wouldn't care about someone.

I have been taking the best care of myself that I can at the moment with the cravings that I have had and I have chosen the lesser of two evils today and that has been ok, there has been no shame cycle and no guilt, I am alive and expressing myself to my fullest capacity.

There is much to integrate and much to pursue here, much to give and much to learn, I am willing to leave the past behind for a future of fresh ideas and Love. I will not give with expectation, for that is based in the ego and serves no one. We are all one and the same and I will forgive myself and walk with Love in my heart for all human beings. Loving kindness expects nothing, for we are all on different levels of our path to enlightenment, we are all valued seekers and we all shall find our way, some are just further along than others and it is my mission to give without question, when I have learnt to do that unquestionably. I am all out of words for tonight.

Thy will be done.

Amen.

Dear God/Goddess,

I feel conflicted about this if this is what I am thinking it is. I have just received the message that it might be sexual energy that is blocked or playing havoc with me and when I think about that I get extremely emotional, like overly emotional. If it is sexual energy I do not have any idea what to do with it or how to channel it let alone think about myself as a sexual being. I remember thinking yesterday that I wanted to be a woman, and what that meant and what that would feel like. I know I am not my authentic self, I am probably far from my authentic self but I am beginning to learn what I want to be I guess. To think about sex well for me I guess I have to break this down into really really small bite sized chunks because this will be painful and this will be difficult. I know I have been tested more than once but I resisted and that is a good thing. I am worthy of forgiveness. I made a conscious decision to stop being sexually active at least 9 months ago and so far it has been successful, I have been sexually aroused by a dream and watched a small amount of porn but never masturbated. I just didn't feel like it was turning me on. I haven't thought about sex for these 9 or so months now because I have no one to think about having sex with. I wish not to think about some random woman I know nothing about and share nothing with, I have no partner and have no desire for sex without a connection.

I am literally not looking for anyone to have sex with ever again, if that has passed for me then so be it, nothing lost to be honest, but a connection, an honest open connection would be nice.

I feel no need to force anything with anyone anymore, no need to be with someone to fulfil my need of not wanting to be alone or to be desired and needed. I want a connection that I can feel.

I get shy and blush when I think of being intimate with that person I feel connected with, because I would be sharing myself with her. I don't know what will come in the future but I know that I will find a way through it. I learnt to lie about my sexuality from an early age after being bullied and that affected the way my sexual development progressed or didn't progress.

I denied for years that I was a lesbian, having sex with men to satisfy this urge for society to be ok with me, for me to be liked and accepted. So things got tangled and the web of lies became thicker and bigger, nothing was real and everything I did was a lie. I now have to rectify that, I have to reconcile all these feelings and experiences in order to help the World, because if I can help myself I automatically help other people. Peoples thoughts about me are none of my business and if I am not accepted for being a lesbian then I am simply not accepted by that person, it doesn't mean that everyone will hate me, that is there own issue and something they need to deal with.

Thanks for listening. Amen.

Good Morning God/Goddess,

I find myself in the middle of a story, and I have played a role I had no idea I was playing, now I find myself lost without a role, only fragments of memories and parts of stories and shards of the past that really make no sense to me, but there is something greater happening here. Oh and what it is to find yourself the main character of the story. In all the movies, Love prevails, Love always prevails because the power of Love is something special. What happens next in the story? I used to like choose your own adventures when I was a child, but this? This is my life and I am overwhelmed at the enormity of this situation here. I have been more scared of live performance and talking in front of an audience than death itself, and apparently death is final. Living on after a performance seems so much harder with the criticism out there, but I imagine if the cause is big enough one will endure what one must. My story now requires me to participate, to engage with people and learn new things. I must pick and choose the qualities more favourable to myself and find a meaning and purpose behind my actions, and not only that, I must know that people are watching and listening, now whether they are judging for the better or the worst, that is not the issue, so what is the issue Nicole? What is it that most frightens you about this role that you are to play? I know my expectations are high of myself, so I need to relax a lot. I need to have more fun and take things less seriously. Be less critical of yourself, you're doing your best.

You see, well connecting to my body is really hard, I feel things with my body, that is where all the negative data is stored in my cells, I don't know how to release that and move my body and connect to it. I imagine beauty is found when connecting to your own body, I might think perhaps. How do I connect to my body and feel my way through the negativity? How do I release it from my cells and not to pass it on to my children? I don't want them to inherit any of these feelings. I feel like I could be naked in nature, but that would go and get me arrested in todays society, but nature will help, so today I will find some nature and I will ask her to help me heal. I have noticed this morning that my old habit with my eating control thing has come out to play, and I know the food part is the hardest for me to relinquish control of because it has been the longest standing issue

157

and way to soothe myself. Intellectually I mostly see that now, I am sure there is much I am not seeing but emotionally I feel vulnerable today, and I need to explore that desperately. If I just keep talking this all out maybe I will get somewhere.

I am still interested to know why I was more inclined to play a dead person than a living person? For what reason would I have been happy to play that dead person and not someone that is alive and living that has feelings and emotions and desires and wants to create? I actually have a photo of the day I was in drama playing the dead person on a table, like it is shocking to me that I would have wanted that. But what is also shocking is now that I am alive and I want to be alive, who do I want to be and what do I want to do with my life? I cannot plan out everything I know that, I want room for imagination and play but truly what am I going to create? I remember Aunty Linda telling me I could co-create, well what would I want to co-create?

Dear God/Goddess,

Tonight was my good friend Natalie's farewell dinner celebration. It was a good night, dinner and music. I don't like or know how to do goodbyes very well, they are hard and make me confused, but as long as she is happy that is all that matters.

What is going on? I can hear the constant laughter within my head? What am I doing? Where am I going? I know how to drive a car, thats it. What am I doing here? I don't know so much, I tried to dance tonight, I did move my body, I did. I want my friend Natalie to be happy and safe and her human rights upheld, I want all of those things, so why does everyone go out of my life and where do they go? Some days this place makes sense and my purpose here seems crystal clear and other days, like right now anger and confusion take over and it blinds me. Why am I vegetarian? Why Nicole? You are changing all these behaviours and you don't even know why you are doing it. And when people talk to me and ask me questions I freeze especially if they are about me, I don't hate talking about myself but I get tongue tied and don't know what to say. Maybe I haven't thought about it long enough. Why are you making all these changes to your lifestyle Nicole? What is going on for you on a daily basis? What is the point of me writing this down? What is the point in sitting here by myself thinking these thoughts and writing down absolute random irrelevant things? I am missing a lot of the puzzle here and I am confused. I don't know what will make this feel better. I have had days off work and yes I have been unwell but what have I been doing with myself? Processing what? What have I been through? Where have I been? What have I been doing and why have I been doing it? I have had so many people come in and out of my life, is that what happens? Do you just meet people and become friends with them and then they go away? Your sending me messages without giving me the meaning here, what do I do with what this woman said to me? There are two ways to take it and I am not sure how to take it. What is going on and why is it happening? I feel like so confused here. Where has the meaning gone to? I had meaning and purpose the other day, where has that gone? Why do I think I am a soldier of this World and why do I think we are all soldiers? Why would I have thought that?

Why do people make eye contact with me? And why do I have to hold their gaze until they look away first? What does it mean? Why do I make up reasons in my head for all these things that are going on in my head? Am I crazy? Do I still have voices in my head and does God/Goddess talk to me? Who am I? Why am I here? Where am I going? Where have I been? I want to be a writer but I can't write a sentence properly. What is going on? Why is cheese so hard to give up? Why do I run out of things to say when talking to people? Why can't I hold a conversation anymore? Could I ever hold a conversation? Will I ever be able to go on a date longer than 1.5 hours? Is there something wrong with me? If someone answered yes to the last question what would constitute the wrong part? Why couldn't I dance more for Natalie? What did that lady mean when she said that in my ear? Am I supposed to get on stage and dance with them? In hindsight was I supposed to do something else? Be spontaneous? How do you be spontaneous? Do you just be spontaneous and not think about it? Did I ruin Natalie's party? Why is all this going through my head? For what reason am I writing this down when I will never read it again? Why do I keep a journal anyway? What are these words and how do I know them? How do I retain these words in my brain and use them meaningfully? I am angry with myself and I am shocked and disappointed. I want food. I am not finished here though, I haven't gotten enough out, there is still so much inside of me that I am stuck here, typing useless, pointless information that has no purpose or use or meaning. I don't know so much, how do I get by? How do I seriously get by in this World? How did I get my car licence? How did I get a job? How did I finish High School? How have I done all that? Where have I been since then? What have I been doing? Which reality have I been in? I have not been of this World? Have I been somewhere else? Fighting something or someone or something. None of this makes sense and now this computer is playing up. Where am I? In this moment where am I? Do I exist? If I exist in what world do I exist? I want food, I am hungry and I want Mc Donald's. I'm out.

Give me strength please Goddess/God, please I am asking you to help guide me in this moment because I feel overwhelmed with energy I cannot contain. I need guidance and time to work through all this please. I need wisdom and grace to get through these moments please. I want food please. Thats what I need and want. Thank you kindly.

Thy will be done.

Amen.

Good Morning All,

I must start with yesterday's "Day of Doubt", that was intense and somewhat scary I have to admit. I was in a bad place, I purchased horror movies, ate take away and drank beer all while feeling the darkness within me. The beer didn't help change my mental state at all, it just made my stomach hurt, the horror movies just gave me another perspective and the food was bad for my health but tasty. I got 24 minutes through the first movie and I just couldn't handle it anymore. How does torture and punishment bring about a new way of seeing the World? It doesn't, at all. Scaring someone into change doesn't work, it is not the answer, it is cruel and inhumane and against what I believe to be true healing. True healing involves compassion and loving kindness and listening and beauty and transformation.

I ask of the God/Goddess and my Angels to help dissolve any intolerant anger, any violent anger that I hold within myself please, it is not useful and serves no purpose anymore. I can protect myself in other ways. The anger I need is the passionate anger, the one that transforms things, not the violent lash out and hurt others, or the anger that doesn't understand someone else's motives, I must replace this anger with something please, so your guidance and wisdom here would be greatly appreciated. I will immerse myself in nature today and show myself that beauty is all around me and that I am beauty.

My first instinct is to say sorry about yesterday but I won't, I will take from it the lessons needed for me to progress. I am becoming more conscious of my need to apologise for things and myself, so I am getting better. I don't think I have been really noticing the good I have been achieving lately. I think I have been growing and trying hard but not acknowledging it very well, so here I sit today and I must say that I feel like I can achieve something great.

When I know where I belong, I know myself. How beautiful is that?

How does one find belonging? I imagine that I want to belong in this body first, because I have been disconnected from it for so long, that is the first place I want to belong, for without knowing my body I know nothing of my rights or myself. I want to belong to my tribe, my family tribe, I want to belong to that tribe. I want to belong to a friendship group, another sort of tribe, a collection of people. I want to belong to that. I want to belong to a greater tribe, the tribe of humanity, where beauty lies, where art comes from and collaboration and peace can come from. I want to belong to the tribe of humanity where we work together, team work, where we share with each other. But first I imagine I must belong to this body and connect with my soul.

This body holds me, it is shaped as it is shaped, I have the choice to change that shape but I wont, I don't wish to, I don't have that desire. The shape that I am is the shape that I have been created in and that is perfect, because we are created from perfect Love. I want to belong to this body, to feel the way it works, to behold its beauty of creativity in the way in which it works. The systems of which it is made of, oh the splendour. With this belonging to this body that I was born into I was given rights, something that I can only truly possess if I inhabit my body fully and totally with love and kindness and belonging, with ownership.

I care for my possessions well, I have noticed that, for example my cd's would be something I am very particular about, because they give my life joy, passion, I care for them and have no issues telling people around me to treat them with respect, because I care for them, but what of this body of mine? I have let men have my body for much less than a beer, and do with it what they will, but not my cd's, how strange. What a strange concept. I have allowed my body to endure pain for the pleasure of others, but not my cd's, for the music seemed a lot more important than my body and my dignity. How strange that is. That is not what I want for anyone else, woman or man, our bodies are sacred and more important than possessions, we just must find our ways to connect with these things instead of the possessions on the outside of us.

I want to belong in my body because I want to feel what embodying those rights feels like. I want that experience please. I ask nothing more than that, because I have heard that is our birth right, that is something we are born to do, we just don't know how to do it yet, so lets start to learn, lets start to try and see what one must do to belong to the body. I want to feel movement without judgement within my own head. I want to feel power within my movements, a sacred power that demands nothing but being felt and experienced for what it is. I want to own my movements without judgements and second guessing myself. I want a lot and I am sure it is all worth it, it has value, these ideas Nicole, and we shall all make it to this place, I am sure of that.

We shall find our ways.
The light shines in us all.
Thy will be done.

Amen.

Good Evening All,

I want to know you, I don't want to lay in the middle of nowhere and think about what you might be all thinking. This is a difficult place to be sometimes, deep intense moments of realisation, something shocking then something enlightening, somewhat bizarre, but the God and Goddess only give you what you can handle. I realise now that my self imposed hate on myself has caged me and made my hate grow towards others, and that is not my desire. I am a being of great Love, like others, I know that. I will take the path less traveled now, because the old way wasn't working and I want something beautiful for us all. I must trust others, the universe and myself and I will be fine. I am capable of doing this and providing the basic things in life for myself, I guess the hard part is finding that worthiness and the ability to weather the loneliness. But we are so strong, we endure much and we don't even realise it. When I once said we were all soldiers I was right. I know that, because we are all fighting a war, within ourselves and within our community, the war is multilayered and deep but I know there are solutions to these problems. I could drive back to Melbourne and live, study and work there, but what would that achieve but another brick in the wall. I must find the courage to step off that ledge and face death head on, for I know the reason why. I remember the reason why, I can feel the reason, smell the reason why, and I have memories of the reason that through everything have not gone or faded, they have remained with me and I can see her smile and see her hands playing the piano, I am telling you there is nothing more beautiful or magical as that. Well there is a lot of things that rock my World but those few things would be the finest of them all.

I am what you would call completely on my own in a physical sense, I have no company, no one to talk to, no phone, no contact with the outside World except for strangers and that has been minimal so far, so I am alone, but I have cleared my heart and mind enough to get enough Peace for over 7 hours driving with no music or no radio, so no stimulation other than my own mind and ideas and being as present as possible. Do I feel lonely? No I don't, when I hear the birds for example I take pure joy in hearing their miracle sounds, their miracle existence. I don't feel alone because I talk

165

to myself, it helps me work things out, it starts a dialogue and it becomes cathartic and reflective and at times rather humorous. I just make things up, I make meaning out of nothing with my imagination I guess. But it must come from somewhere so I guess I am not making it up, I am just a radio station for a crossed line, because there is good and bad influences here and I have to decipher which one is which, with Logic and reason I guess.

I am just rambling now.

So mote it be.

Good Evening God/Goddess,

I am asking for the strength to ride this wave please, I am feeling nervous and my anxiety is intense. I know that I will never know whats going on, I just want to live. I feel like I am shaking internally, my hands are shaking and I am jittery. I don't know what is going to happen but I am hopeful for the future. I find it helpful to wave and acknowledge the people driving on the other side of the road, it is some sort of connection in a place where there is just land and not many people. A nice man stopped and asked me how I was and I was struggling but I appreciated the concern. I am now inside "Spuds Roadhouse" in South Australia, 500 and something kms away from Coober Pedy, and thats weird because my Dad used to call me Spud and I don't know if that has something to do with my feelings. I know when the wave is good it is good and I enjoy it but when it is difficult I struggle, but I know there is a reason I am feeling this way and I have faith that I can get through it. With your grace Dear Goddess/God I will get through this feeling and with your Love. I am kind of feeling like I am scared of something, like dying maybe but I am not sure. But it is a fear of sorts and a doubt. I had a plan before now I am doubting it and I don't want to doubt it, because if my plan worked I would be happy and alive. So I will just ride these moments out and think of others that are struggling too, that we are in this together, that none of us are alone, no matter what!

So I have been mentally ill, I have been diagnosed with many different diagnoses and now I have left everything behind, pills and all to start a spiritual journey back to my soul. Where do I go from here? What do I do? How do I do things that are right? And who is Spud anyway?

Who am I? What am I doing here? The energy here is provoking serious anxiety within me, I feel uncomfortable, but I am ok, I will survive this feeling. If I acknowledge it and allow it to flow over me then I can move forward. There is immense beauty in this world, in the details, in the smallest things that I have noticed. Like ants, they are strong. There is meaning in that, I cannot explain myself at this moment but there is meaning there. Why is this called Spuds Roadhouse? This place is making me very uncomfortable that is for sure. I am craving hot chips so bad, like my mouth is watering for them and my stomach is rumbling and feels like I am starving for them.

So this "Spiritual Journey" began yesterday, 19/10/2018, and I have driven from Footscray, Melbourne, Victoria to Spud's Roadhouse in Pimba, South Australia. I have no idea how many kilometres that is nor how long it has taken me time wise, all I know is that I am processing things, good and bad, light and dark. I don't know where I have been, but I have known some amazing people, and I am sure I will know some more amazing people, I guess I just have to ride out this feeling.

My wounded child and my addicted self are doing well, resting and enjoying the silence and calm. We have enough food and water and we are warm/cool and comfortable.

What do I do with all this writing I have accumulated? All the questions and all the stuff that has happened within my mind? Where do I put it? How do I use it for good? Do I put it out into the World? I want to. I want people to read it, for whatever reason that is.

I am getting flashes of things into my mind with feelings and sensations, what do these things mean? I have moments where I appoint meaning to them but sometimes I am shocked at what they could actually mean.

There have been so many mixed messages within my life, and I know I fell at times but my heart has Love in it, that much I know, so I will not lose sight of that now in this moment when I am slightly fearful. I ground myself within my beautiful body and tell myself I am safe. I look around and notice that I am not in the past or future, I am in the now, sitting at a table typing on a computer. My feet are in shoes with no socks and my feet are flat against the floor. I am safe, I am secure.

Loving Kindness: I send out a prayer to All, to All Souls, May You be Safe, May You be Well, May You be Happy, May Your Human Rights be upheld.

Thank you kindly for listening.

Thy will be done.

So mote it be.

Good Evening God/Goddess,

I had a dream, there was a fire and I had to get my cats out but I couldn't find them. Then when I was coming back up the stairs there were half eaten hearts that had been vomited up by a wolf, or a dog I think, and there were also whole hearts as well. There was a lot of blood and it was a little gruesome. Someone was trying to clean it up and I just moved it aside and walked back up the stairs. There were people in this room and they were playing games and I yelled and became so enraged and scared 3 of the women. They were so scared of me that they couldn't even look into my eyes or at my face at all. They eventually looked at me again but it felt like pure wrath and the feeling I get when thinking about it doesn't make me feel good.

The running up the stairs past the half eaten hearts and whole hearts is probably symbolic of the people I have hurt and left behind maybe? I don't like the wrath that I felt and the fact that I have hurt people doesn't help, but that is life I imagine.

On another thought, if I was to surrender these diary entries what am I hoping to achieve from it? Am I telling a story? What would the purpose be of having these notes made public? Is there anything of value in here? If people purchased all of it as a book what would be taken from it? Do I read through all the entries and change things? No because then authenticity is lost. If you are to take the risk you take it wholeheartedly.

What am I doing? I am driving half way across Australia to an unknown destination with no real plan, what on Earth am I doing? I have no idea what I am doing but something is guiding me forward so just relax Nicole.

I must say I have thoroughly enjoyed driving the explorers way highway through the middle of Australia, it has felt so amazing, I have felt free. The Sun has been shining on my skin, the wind in my hair and feeling as if my every need is being met. I am fed and watered, it is visually stunning and the clean air is stunning. I was clean, comfortably dressed and had choices up my sleeve. I pulled over and rested, time has become an irrelevant concept, I had to be nowhere by a particular time, I had no dead lines, no bills due, I am not paying taxes but I was waving at nearly everyone I drove past. The feeling of not having to think about a clock and time is absolutely liberating, the stress free nature of it is something you cannot compare to anything. I am staying in an underground motel in Coober Pedy, Outback South Australia, something I have wanted to do for a while now, so as I travel along the way I am finding out more things I want to do and I am doing them. I went for a walk and stood on a lookout today with a view as beautiful as anything I have ever seen and it was just land, no city, no buildings, only a few shops and houses around so not many people but this vast open land. It was stunning. I went in and had a look at an underground opal museum, very nice. It seems if I follow my intuition it leads me to places I need to be and indeed want to be.

I am staying in a motel tonight and need to check out by 10am the next morning and I have no phone for an alarm so I hope I wake up. It is so strange having no phone and no watch, no way to tell the time. So what does it mean to have no concept of time? It makes the day longer and fuller I think, the now is so deep and refreshing that it feels like eternity. When you can free your mind of hate and past mistakes the present moment can be the most amazing thing.

I noticed that when I think about the past I become uncomfortable and a little anxious and when I think about the future I become anxious as well but if I stay in the present, connected to my intuition and listening to my heart I am calm and buoyant, light. This process of letting go of control is and has been difficult but it feels good and I am sure it is going to feel better the more and more I trust in it.

I ask of the Goddess/God to help me find a way to build my confidence within myself because the doubts I have about myself can become overwhelming and I lose all perspective of myself.

I have literally walked out of my old life and driven away, with no plans to fix what has happened and to walk away from all I had built up until that point. I left two cats in a unit that I paid for by working for Toll. I saved some money and I am now living off that, I feel rich in my spirit but my bank account in dwindling and I have no place of residence and no contact with any friends or family. This is a big thing it feels like. My unit was fully furnished, unclean and I just left, walked away with two bags, two pillows, a blanket, a car, my inner child and my addicted self and my social worker self. I have accumulated nothing but food for the journey and I have cleaned out the boot of my car with more items ready to be binned. All I can say to myself is I have no idea what I am doing but it feels pretty amazing right now. The silence has been golden, something stunning to behold. Last night alone in the car, the sky was shining with stars and the moon was shining brightly, no sounds, maybe a passing car but other than that, pure silence. Liberating.

I am noticing needs as they arise and fulfilling them myself, I simply talk to myself and go through a checklist of what I might need at any given moment or whether my emotions have become unbalanced and I am craving something other than what I think I want. For example with food in particular if I notice that I want food in my head but not my body, my stomach is saying I am full then maybe I am craving something else, to be soothed because an emotional need is unfulfilled, like I am getting lonely or anxious or sad. So then I just problem solve a way through another list of possible solutions to the problem, like drinking water if I am craving food, or having a nap if I am able to do so. Going for a walk, no matter how short is always a good one and being as mindful while walking as possible. I talk to myself in my head as well. I start a dialogue, in a most positive way as I can and I just problem solve the situation. I created these lists of solutions when thinking about things that soothed me when I was younger, what activities soothed me and captured my attention, made me feel good. I think along the way of growing up we lose our imagination, it becomes stifled by the layers of mud that we get covered in, issues and past hurts. Thats what it has felt like for me anyway. But for some reason there was always a voice in the back of my head that said I need help, all I need is some help. And there must of been part of me that thought I was worthy of this help because I don't think I have ever given up trying to help myself. I have been to numerous detoxes, I have been to rehab on more than one occasion, I was involved with Spectrum for over 2 years. I have investigated 12 step programs and read many books on mental health and people's recovery journeys, so I know I have tried hard to get well, so I can commend myself on the effort.

I have a great memory for the mistakes that I have made but not much memory for the good I have done. I know that I have tried my hardest in all situations. I have given up on many things but tried hard on many things too. I literally have no idea what I have been doing for the past 14/15 years but I know that I have met a lot of amazing people. I know that the Lord/Lady know what I have and haven't done and what I am doing now is a test and part of my contract. I have agreed to do something before I was born and I am living it out now, I guess I just need to enjoy and trust.

Why can't I see I am meant to exist? I am obviously meant to be alive because I know I have had many moments of where I was in a very risky situation where my life could have ended or I could have been hurt more than I have been. Where are all these thoughts coming from? From where are they created and why do they get expressed the way they do?

I am rambling and have found myself in a place of needing to stop talking because nothing I have left to say would be useful or interesting.

Thank you kindly for the shoulder to vent on dear Lord/Lady, I am outies.

Thy will be done.

So mote it be.

Dear Lord/Lady,

This is a journey of forgiveness, a journey to reclaim my soul and your Love. I must claim my birth rights and express to the World the clear message that we are all worth it, that we are the currency of the World, we have the value here. I am experiencing doubts about the journey a little, and I guess that is understandable but these doubts are telling me to turn back. I wish not to turn back now, although the road ahead is mostly dark, there is some light shining through in the shape of some ideas about what to do and where to go. I guess the hardest thing is to release the fear and doubt completely and trust and enjoy the journey I am on.

I feel connected to the landscape around me, the red dirt and bush and scrub. The fact that I have seen Eagles on this journey when I didn't even know they existed within Australia. This is the country I was born in and I know nothing about it, that still blows my mind.

There is no one around, it is silent and it is tranquil here. I don't know what this journey requires but I am sure I will develop the necessary attributes along the way or discover I had them all along.

I must say though, that my doubts are creating a fall back story in my head about if I found myself somewhere along the way, and I panic and think to myself I have made a massive mistake then I would just put it down to "mental illness". But that doesn't seem right anymore. Something is different, something has changed.

I literally know not what I have done in the past so I am choosing to move forward with faith that I am not mentally ill and that these choices I am making are for the best. I know I get stuck in my ego trying to intellectualise these issues while I know that these are issues of the heart and I must feel my way through them. So here I go, here goes nothing and everything. Here I am setting sail to a place unknown, maybe it just might be "The Most Beautiful Place I Have Ever Seen". I want that, I want that for us all.

Thy will be done.

So mote it be.

Good Day Dear Lord/Lady and All,

What an amazing day. That walk was phenomenal, such beauty, such deep meaning behind their stories. For example, stories were the children's inheritance, like that concept just blows my mind, I literally don't have the words to describe what that means to me. I had some profound insights along that track and I am sure I will remember them when I need them but the story aspect of the Indigenous culture is so beautiful, it feels like the lifeblood of culture.

This was a journey I took both my Father and Mother on today, and I am eternally grateful that they are in my heart and walking right next to me. I cannot thank them enough for all they have given me.

Along the way I am noticing people's names that I once knew from primary school, like I stayed at the Radika underground motel in Coober Pedy, which reminds me of Primary School and the good people I shared it with. And the name Reza on a number plate. I saw the name Jez today on a number plate which was one of Brodie's ex boyfriends. I saw a woman that reminded me of Tahnee. I feel like all of these people are with me on this journey and it is wonderful.

Today was a celebration of my Dad's 55th Birthday at Uluru, Northern Territory. Tomorrow is the day Natalie flies back to Perth, so I will take her with me to my next destination. Then the day after that it is Astrid's Birthday so where ever I shall be we shall be.

I also noticed the name Kane on a boys t-shirt today, and I remember both Kane's, "Little" Kane and "Big" Kane. They too are on this journey with me. I dreamt of Heath last night which was beautiful. I also remember dreaming of my cousin Sarah and she hugged me which made me so happy. I also remember dreaming of Emily who also gave me a hug which made me so happy. So thank you All to communicating with me along this journey, this is for You All. I couldn't have done it without you, any of this. I Love You All and I am eternally grateful for your time.

I had the most beautiful Love song in my head a lot today, "Annie's Song" by who I am not too sure, but Kirstyn introduced me to this song and it just makes me think of her, Sarah. She was walking with me today.

All these people were walking with me. Brodie was walking without any aid, we just walked together, whether in silence or talking she was there with me.

We are on Aboriginal Land and this place is sacred. We need to acknowledge the Native people of every Land and we need to respect each other. We have rights and they mean something, we must find that meaning!

Healing is absolutely possible, Love will prevail, I Believe that.

Thy will be done.

So mote it be.

Good Evening All,

I cannot say how good I am feeling right now. No drugs have ever made me feel this good. This feeling is something special, natural and it makes me really appreciate what it is to be Alive, because this is what Life feels like. I am writing this really because I remember seeing a number plate with the name Billie on it. I think of her. To anyone struggling with addiction to any drugs or alcohol because it is difficult but we are strong, so strong, like I cannot begin to describe the strength we are capable of. I now think of Claire whom I shared precious moments with. I have seen you in my dreams and for that I am grateful, if I could give you a hug right now I would, that would make me eternally happy. The light shines from within you Claire and I Love you greatly.

When I think of moments with these people I know I have found treasures. I Love you all.

I remember being at High School and giving Maria a hug and I gave her Love in that moment, I remember that. I remember cooking in Home Economics with Gaelin as my partner and how fun it was.

I remember sitting with Brodie and we were holding each others arms, embraced I would say and we were silent looking into a lake, it was night time and it was stunning. I remember that.

I must say that remembering the moments where I have hurt people are becoming easier to experience, not because I care less I don't think, but because I have learnt these strategies to cope with what has happened. I am trying to find my way back to my Soul, find a path to the Goddess/God, to pure Love. I want that for All of us, it is within All of us. The guilt, shame and grief is bearable and it is worth experiencing for the Love it leaves room for is glorious, pure Heaven.

My words have gone to sleep, dreams are calling me. Goodnight.
I send Love, Peace, Joy, Health and Happiness.

Peace, Love, Empathy.

Thy will be done.

So mote it be.

Dear Lord/Lady,

I am experiencing a bad headache and I am noticing that my sense of worry has increased, I am guessing they are related. I am worried about the fact that this is my life, not a holiday, not some moment of insanity, but my life and I have absolutely no idea where I am going. I know thats not necessarily a bad thing but this is the total unknown for me. I am waking up in foreign places and its great don't get me wrong, I am exploring the World and my strength all in one journey, but I must say there is doubt here. If I focus on the main objective which is Love and only Love I guess I cannot go wrong, but there is doubt all the same. I literally left my unit with my cats inside, I left my job, my family, my friends all in search of what? What am I actually doing? Im not on a journey for a couple of weeks here then I just go back home, I have no home, so maybe thats what I am searching for? Is that what it is Nicole? I am getting hints as to what to do, like glimpses of things that I could do, all I know is that I am not going back. So I am alone, alone physically, I have no physical guests coming along the way with me, its different to what goes on in my head and Heart but no one is here with me physically. So what of this place I am in. There seems to be no time and no days because I am not following a schedule. Dates have been important because I have been celebrating people's Birthdays as I go along, but time is irrelevant here, the days are lost to me and the present is rich until I slip into anxiety. I saw a saying on a t-shirt the other day in Coober Pedy to "Dream Bigger", but like how big? What kind of big? Where do I start to Dream? How does someone Dream of becoming the President of the United States of America? How does someone Dream to become a Prime Minister of a country? I cannot even imagine the enormity of a position like that, but that is how real change is made, these people have real power, so why are we still struggling so badly? Could I even Dream of being in a position of power that great? What would someone need to do to achieve that? And is that my God given mission? What is my purpose dear Lord/Lady? That is my question to you? I know these messages come slowly I just need to acquire more patience I guess. What do you know about your mission Nicole? I know I am here to help somehow. In what way are you meant to help? Uphold Human Rights. How can you manage to do this? I am unsure, because at one point I was living in Melbourne becoming a Social Worker, now I am in the Northern Territory with no fixed address. So there is obviously a lot I need to learn from here, so I take it upon myself to surrender myself to the learning process of this mission. My trust will be reinforced day by day when I learn to trust my intuition and my Heart more. I know doubt is necessary and it is useful I guess it can just be a little annoying when it manifests as a headache.

I know Love is the goal and Love is the reason, that I know in my Heart, so I will surrender my worries to you.

Thank you for listening to me once again.

Thy will be done.

So mote it be.

Dear God/Goddess,

I have woken to a silent storm in the skies around Uluru. The low rumble of the Spirits calling to their people, exclaiming to us all that this land is sacred. The lightening shines through the darkness, guiding the thunder to her Children down below. There is nothing to fear here, she is only whispering to us. In moments of illumination I can see clearly, I can feel all that is around me, the wind is still but brushes against my skin to allow life to be known. The darkness is vast and unknown if you allow yourself to be taken away by your thoughts, if you stay within the moment, with the Spirits, they will calm you and give you comfort, they want you to know there is nothing to fear. There is no rain, nothing pure needs to fall and cleanse us because we have the power to do that ourselves. If we listen to the guiding force of our Hearts we will know where to go, it will lead us to places never seen before. Expand your mind and let the cells of your body be purified by Love. No one is more beautiful than You they say, and they say this to every one of us.

Now the rain comes, but she falls delicately upon my feet and head, no more than a few drops at a time, there needs to be no more than that, the power of these few rain drops is immense if you allow the purification to take place. These are the moments of our lives and in these moments we can be free.

Thank you Spirits, God/Goddess and All,

Thy will be done,

So mote it be.

Good Morning Dear God/Goddess,

I had a Dream last night that was sexual in nature but my body felt no feelings towards the particular experience. It was like I experienced the act of having sex with this man with absolutely no connection, I could physically feel the motions of the act itself but I couldn't feel it within my Heart, deeper within myself. It was completely unsatisfying and there was no bond after, before or during the act. There is something inside me telling me symbolically having sex with a man in my waking life was a total denial of my authentic self, it was a way to deny who I am because I didn't want to accept that part of me that had feelings for women. That itself was a learnt issues, I didn't grow up that way, I grew up thinking about simply kissing a woman, about the soft touch of her skin against mine. I grew up to learn that denial was a way of survival, I survived denying a great part of me and that was my ability to truly connect and Love another human being. I don't know why I keep dreaming of having sex with men, perhaps there is a part of me that is still scared to admit that I want to be intimate with a woman. I am single now and made the conscious choice last year to remain single and not have sex with anyone because I wouldn't want any more intimate experiences to be inauthentic. I am not saying that all my past intimate experiences I wasn't there with Love, but I will admit something was missing, and these relationships ended and I don't want to hurt anyone anymore, because I know I have in the past using sex as a means to feel wanted and good about myself. That is not what I want in an intimate relationship, I want connection and trust and exploration and respect. I want an authentic experience where an orgasm isn't the goal of the experience, the experience is about learning about someones sacred body, about being kind to one another, knowing that we care and at any moment if someone was to become uncomfortable the other would smile and know that in that moment there is only Love and Respect and the knowledge of boundaries and space.

I remember as a small child, because I knew at a young age that I was a lesbian, or that I wanted to be intimate with women not men, that there was something powerful in the simple expression of a kiss. I have been thinking of my lips recently actually and I was looking in a mirror at them and noticed the thought that they were too small and out of proportion in relation to the rest of my face, but then I wondered what are my lips there for? For what purpose do I have these lips? And my thoughts went to two things, one, the power to express Love with the intimate kiss with the one you Love, two they are the portal to your voice, the inner part of you that is sacred, that needs to be expressed. In the moments after realising these two things, which are powerful and beautiful I became able to like my lips for the first time, they had meaning, they had a purpose, their expressions became illuminated to me. I looked at myself in the mirror and told myself that my lips were beautiful.

I am trying to do that with my body as well, find the parts of me that I don't seem to like and find something meaningful behind them and find gratitude for their existence, because denial of the innate beauty of our bodies leads to destruction of ourselves, not just the mental hell we put ourselves through but the moments where we as human beings make the choice to physically alter something so natural and beautiful with things like plastic surgery. There are parts of me that I would consider having surgery on, to "improve" myself, but my Heart tells me not to do this, to be natural and learn to Love everything about myself just the way it is. There is a story behind every scar I have on this body of mine, a story and meaning behind every tattoo, a story and meaning behind the fact that I don't like the excess skin on my upper arms, but if I deny these parts of me I just create more hate and dislike and I don't want to share that with anyone, and my body doesn't deserve to be hated for that, it deserves Respect. If I went through a list of the things I really do not like about my body I would say my upper arms make me feel uncomfortable, my breasts make me feel uncomfortable and my inner thighs and the weight around my hips and waist. Those are the areas that I feel most self conscious about. I used to hate these areas, but I have moved through that hate to a place of feeling uncomfortable with them. You see I look at it this way, my Grandmother had upper arms like mine and I didn't hate her arms, I didn't look at her and think "She is disgusting", that never came into my mind, thats not how I judged my Grandmother, so why should I judge myself like that? And if I am judging myself like that am I simply judging my Grandmother as well? And how does putting that judgement upon my

Grandmother make me feel? I came to understand that my Grandmother grew up working in a cake shop and these were hard times where food wasn't available and it would have been hard to keep a healthy diet, and she struggled with her diet for many years, if not all her life, so this is how she came to find herself with the excess skin on her upper arms, she would have been overweight then lost weight and the excess skin became a part of her, but I don't hate that part of her, I don't judge her on the fact that this happened the way it did, in reality if I think about it now it made her more Beautiful, because she may not of liked that part of herself but she never stopped wearing Beautiful dresses and the smile on her face never went away. So why do I judge myself so harshly when in fact I too have struggled with my weight for a long time, I have been under weight and over weight and absolutely hated myself in both periods of time, so why should I judge myself so harshly? I know I feel uncomfortable with my breasts because I feel like they are sagging and they are, that is just the reality of the situation but I compare myself to other woman. I think my breasts aren't beautiful, when they are because they are mine and again it comes down to the fact that I struggled with my weight, so much so I was underweight there for a period of time and didn't have breasts at all, I didn't even need to wear a bra, I was flat chested, then things changed and I gained a lot of weight and became overweight which meant that my breasts grew quickly from nothing to something quite big, but as I began to lose weight again to become probably the size I am today, which I am pretty damn happy with, my breasts lost the elasticity and bounce and some days more than others I feel uncomfortable about them. I must remind myself that breasts are not primarily a sexual thing, and if I take that sexual aspect out of them I can see they are something that feeds a life you can create, and there is absolutely nothing more powerful than that, so why do I judge my breasts so harshly when their purpose is to feed the life force to our children? It is the most natural process I could think of, animals do it with no thoughts about sex, it is a period of bonding and moments of life affirming action between two life forms, to me that is some powerful stuff right there. More uncomfortable than the feeling of sagging breasts for me is the fact that I cannot ever breast feed, at least I don't think I can. I don't think I have the capacity to do that anymore after I cut open both my nipples to remove nipple rings that were growing out and painful. So that is more disheartening to me I guess than the feeling of sagging breasts. As for my inner thighs, I can deal with them, its just me again comparing myself to other women with firm thighs, there is nothing actually wrong with my thighs at all, they are part of my legs that work perfectly well to get me around from place to place, so I am blessed really to have the body I do. If I remove the lust/sexual part of the whole situation then my body is an amazing set of systems that work in harmony with each other giving me the blessing of experiencing feelings like Love and Gratitude, Enjoyment and Laughter.

I made a pact with myself last year, in 2017 to stay celibate, so that included no sex with any person and no masturbation and it has gone well, I haven't had the desire to have sex with anyone, and I have only had the desire to masturbate once, and I didn't do it because the desire just wasn't strong enough. I don't have the desire to have sex anymore if having sex means reaching an orgasm, I have the desire to share a connection with a woman, to be intimate and learn about each other, to feel something inside of me when I simply touch her skin. Anyway I have rambled here, but I think there is something within me that is coming out in my Dreams about denial and how having sex with a man feels like a complete denial of who I am and who I want to be with and what that looks and feels like to me.

Thank you kindly for listening to me.

Eternal Love.

Good Afternoon Lord/Lady,

We have reached our destination for today, Kings Canyon Resort. Anne Marie, Kirstyn and myself are here relaxing in the shade, sipping tea and listening to the bird folk. I had many a thoughts while travelling down here, but one subject that really affected me was the memory of a man I knew from a caravan park in Brooklyn, Melbourne. The notorious Half Moon Caravan Park. This man's name was Lionel, he has now passed away tragically from hitting his head when passing out from being so drunk, but what struck me about this man was the absolute lack of care there was in his life. I can't recall if he had family, but he never had visitors, friends or family come to see him for that matter. He lived alone in a filthy caravan in the middle of the park up the back, hidden away. His crime? As far as I can remember he had sex with a minor, but he thought it was consented but he was charged and spent time in prison. He was not given the opportunity of rehabilitation he was just put in jail, did his time then put in this caravan park to die. Now some may say he deserved it for what he did, but I saw the way this man lived. He lived in his own urine, faeces and blood. He had burns on the soles of his feet, blisters full of fluid, from getting so drunk, passing out with the heater on that he couldn't feel his skin burning. He smoked those chop chop cigarettes and drank as much as he took breaths, he literally wanted to die but obviously couldn't bring himself to the choice point of killing himself in one go. He was committing suicide slowly, painfully and what looks like punishing himself for something that looked like it plagued his mind. No one lives like that when they care about themselves, they live like that because they hate themselves, they hate something they have done, they want to die, and this man, he wanted to die. Why had the Police and Justice system failed this man too? Why does a human being that made a mistake have to die in such an undignified way? He confessed his mistakes, but he was never given the opportunity of help. Is there not help out there for people that have issues of these sorts?

I have had so many people confide in me, both male and female that they have been sexually abused, so it is obviously a major major issue, and it affects all of society whether people want to see it that way or not. Firstly we just assume that the perpetrator wouldn't feel shame because the crime is so hard to intellectually make sense of. Secondly it affects the survivor, and any single person that survivor comes into contact with, because we are all connected and the energy and peoples behaviour affects us whether we are aware of it or not. The survivor can hold onto some serious hate and shame and pass that on, unknowingly to any person that they start any relationship with. Our moods and behaviour and attitudes and comments and silences affect each other.

Lionel's victim, or person that went through trauma didn't deserve to have that happen, that is the truth, but neither did Lionel deserve to live in a self induced prison of shame that ended his life.

I am trying to look at this from another perspective, to try and see things from another angle to see if there is a solution to this issue, because if there is a solution we need to find it sooner rather than later, for every future generation of children to come.

I have witnessed the movements of the #MeToo campaign where women are speaking their truths and telling their stories and that is an amazing thing to see, what a cathartic and inspirational thing to do. These people need to be held accountable, absolutely, but we need Justice here too, we need to find healing solutions to the issues not just sweep it under the rug and let it keep happening with all this hate in our Hearts, it is tearing us down and killing us.

There needs to be programs of empowerment for people that have suffered trauma, programs to teach children boundaries and emotional intelligence. This issue is something that is close to my Heart. I suffered with mental health issues and maybe it was psychosis, but this was as real as anything I have ever experienced. I couldn't come to terms with the shame. I wanted death to take me away because thats what I thought I deserved. I couldn't find any Love within me, no matter what anyone told me about myself. That is my shadow side, that is my darkest deepest shame. This is not an intellectual concept to be nutted out, this is an emotional issue that needs to be felt out by all those people that have suffered.

I literally have lost myself in this entry, I feel as if I am making no sense and I am defending people that need help rather than punishment, because it is proven, time and time again that punishment isn't deterring this behaviour, there needs to be another solution, there needs to be more discussions about what these unwell people need to be rehabilitated.

For the children, for all the children, we need to change what is happening with this issue, because if we don't then nothing will change and I just cannot stand the thought of this continuing to happen when we can really make a change. It will be hard, but the hard things in life are worth it.

Eternal Love,
Nicole Marie Halls.

Dear Goddess/God and All,

I am six days into a journey into the unknown. I just had a profound experience walking down the road heading straight towards a storm, in the dark of night, alone, along the side of the road. As I was walking I saw a figure in front of me, now because there was not much light at first I thought I may be hallucinating, but upon focusing my eyes better I saw it was a Dingo coming towards me. It was walking straight towards me and I will admit fear entered my mind and I didn't know what to do. I am not sure about Dingoes, they are wild dogs but do they hurt people? As it kept approaching me I stepped back and bent down and picked up a rock and threw it in its direction and it ran into the bushes. So I started walking back towards camp, where it was safe I imagine, but I did keep looking around behind me to check if it was coming, and it was following me, indeed. I had a larger rock in my hand ready to throw at it just in case, but when I noticed it was still following me I turned right around and faced it, looked at it and it went off into the bushes not to be seen again. I want to know what this meant, was this Dingo trying to connect with me? Was it dangerous or curious? I was fearful but curious, but obviously more fearful than curious, also because of the lack of light I really wasn't sure what to do. When arriving back to the camp I headed for a shower but kept noticing a thought saying this is an exercise in trust, and that has been repeating in my head a lot today actually, trust, trust.

I was walking straight into this storm, I wanted to see how close I could get to really appreciate its beauty, and while it was beautiful this Dingo scared me. I know I will process this and a lesson will crystallise in my mind.

I am six whole days gone from my old life complete and I have let go of my cats better than I would have thought, but I know I gave them all the Love I had and space they needed to go onto their next Homes, where ever that may be. I have left behind my dependence on my Family and Friends and I am in a situation where I am totally relying on myself. There is no one else here but me to make decisions, to direct the course of actions I take, the road ahead is endless with possibilities if I stay in the present and focused on the fact that Love is guiding me and if I follow my Heart I cannot fail. I know that I am resourceful, I have proven that before when doing things for others, so it is now time to use my skills to navigate through the challenges that lie ahead.

Learning to Love myself is a massive part of this journey, as is being able to find trust in other people, trust in myself and trust in the universe. And that process takes time and it feels so uncomfortable I must admit but I have been making an effort today to do small things that allow my trust to develop. Also I have to believe in myself, for if I don't believe in myself who can I believe in? I know I have received so many nice words and messages of Love from so many good people, but I just didn't believe them, I just couldn't feel it within myself. So here I sit in the middle of the desert contemplating all that comes into my mind. My days are my own and I am quite content in communicating with nature and the higher powers around me, the days feel longer because time isn't an issue, I have no time limitations upon me and decisions are easier to make. I don't feel pressured at all and I stop and nap when necessary. I do think a lot, when driving long distances I don't listen to music and I didn't listen to the audio book today I just thought and thought and thought until I exhausted myself out. I am rambling about nothing now because I am not tired and I feel a bit restless, but I will go now and relax into the night and Dream about somewhere over the rainbow.

Eternal Love,
Eternally Grateful,
Nicole Marie Halls.

Good Evening Goddess/God and All,

I walked Kings Canyon today and it was an amazing feeling to reach the top. The steep peaks had amazing, breath taking views and my camera could not capture the absolute perfection of the moment. I went a little off course today and became fearful I would get lost, but if I think about it now am I already lost in this whole situation, trying to find something unknowable? I went off track and found myself looking over my shoulder with hesitation that I would get lost, but I kept on moving forward and followed the signs in a totally unfamiliar direction towards the unknown again. I kept moving forward so that was a good thing. I didn't recognise the ground upon which I walked so I made a plan in my head of what I should do if I got stuck there for the night and once I had decided on the alternative plan I had problem solved in my head, the track then became familiar again and I was heading back down from where I came. I didn't let the fear consume me and I didn't turn around and go back. I kept moving forward and trusted my new plan with a little doubt still in my awareness but I did not let it conquer me. I noticed when the fear was present I lost all ability to really view the beauty of the situation I was in. I was in Kings Canyon, a place of history and significance and such perfect beauty and I lost the ability to feel and see the magnificence because fear was present. As I said it didn't overwhelm me and stop me from moving forward but it did affect me. When I realised I was back on the path towards the car, the beauty returned and probably became even more beautiful.

The sign at the beginning of the walk said it would take two hours return but it honestly felt like half an hour that I walked, even when I got lost too. Time doesn't feel limiting out here, it is freeing and boundless. I have trouble even trying to describe the way it feels not having to be anywhere on time, or waiting for anything to begin or finish. Every minute I have had these last 7 days have been mine and mine alone and I have driven for hours but it seems like nothing. I made it to Alice Springs today, yay! This is now my new home for some time, I don't know how long and I don't know where I will stay but I will go into town tomorrow and discover what I can. I am living by the Gandhi quote, "Be the Peace you want to see in the world."

Time wanders through me as thoughts consume me,
I can feel the layered history of this place and these people,
Guide me along this journey with Peace behind me,
And may forgiveness fall at my feet daily.

Thy will be done.

So mote it be.

Good Afternoon Lord/Lady,

I don't know what this feeling is and it is making me very uncomfortable. I am almost feeling angry and I cannot understand why. I don't know what to do with this energy.

Everything and Everyone I have experienced has led me to this moment. I am waking up to realise I am in a Dream, the People I have met have taught me things I have needed to know. But what does it All mean? This moment I am experiencing right now is enormous and it is heavy. What of this moment? What am I doing? I intellectually understand that the meaning is derived from the journey and the moments of experiencing, not the destination, but what of this heavy feeling I am experiencing now? What is it? I cannot quite understand what it is, so I will ride it out the best I can. There is nowhere I can run to anymore, no destructive habits that can soothe this moment, I must sit here and write or draw and feel it out without judgement.

I have been experiencing memories of when I have caused harm to another human being and it causes internal distress, but there is nothing I can do to run from it anymore. I don't want to die, at all, I want to Live, but what will become of me? Where will I go and what will I do? I thought I had a plan back in Melbourne, I thought I was building a Life. This doesn't feel "wrong" so to speak it just feels foreign. I am feeling a little guilt for leaving my old Life behind, abandoning my Cats, Family and Friends, but I feel deep down this is what I am meant to be doing. This trust thing is a difficult one but I am trying my best. I want to trust, wholeheartedly in fact, I guess I just need to do this slowly.

I am doing some artwork at the moment because I want to turn this uncomfortable feeling into something beautiful. I want to transform this inner turmoil from negative to positive, something I can admire and share one day. I want to see and experience the most Beautiful thing in the World, that something that I Dreamed of one night that is hiding somewhere in my unconscious. Apart from meeting the most Beautiful Woman in the World already, and sharing Time with Her, I want to see what this other Beautiful thing is, I want to see it manifest, I want to see it grow, whatever it may be.

I have no more words today, so thank you for listening once again.

Eternal Gratitude,
Eternal Love,
Nicole Marie Halls.

Good Evening God/Goddess and All,

I couldn't shake this heavy uncomfortable feeling today, I think I may be getting my period but I am unsure.

I got a new tattoo today and I Love it, its simple but grand and I took some awesome photos with it in them today. I am going to get some amazing photos with this tattoo and what it represents. Its simply the word Love tattooed across my knuckles. So simple but so profound. That and my Bamboo are my favourite.

1 Year = 365 Days
10 Years = 3650 Days
3650 Days = 87,600 Hours
87,600 Hours = 5,256,000 Minutes
5,256,000 Minutes = 315,360,000 Seconds

So these numbers or amount of Time is only relevant for one single reason, thats the approximate amount of Time since I last saw or heard of Sarah. I have not known Her longer than I knew Her but I still cannot shake the Feelings she produces. I think roughly I was Her friend for approximately 7 years, and 10 years have gone by since I spoke to Her again on Facebook, so thats a total of 17 years I have held in the way that I Feel. It is only until recently I have even gained the Courage to write down how I Feel.

17 Years = 6205 Days
6205 Days = 148,920 Hours
148,920 Hours = 8,935,200 Minutes
8,935,200 Minutes = 536,112,000 Seconds

That is the approximate amount of Time I have been avoiding how I Feel about this Woman.

Why did I avoid telling someone the Truth for so long? I know, because my Love was motivated my selfish reasons, I wanted Her to return the Love and I was so scared of rejection that I kept quiet. But what of the experiences of not telling Her? I wanted to die for so long even though I didn't tell Her. I thought rejection would kill me but not telling Her the Truth was killing me far greater. I know that everything that has happened has happened for a reason, I am grateful for that, for every moment I have been given and from this moment onwards, and All moments prior. I guess the greatest lesson from that is to tell the Truth, no matter how I think it will make me feel, because not telling the Truth nearly destroyed me, it nearly ended my Life. And what of hiding Love Nicole? What was wrong with your Love?

I learnt my Love was disgusting and "wrong" so I conformed to societies ways, but found myself breeding a feeling of resentment and hate that I must forgive myself for now.

Millions of Seconds have passed since I have seen Her face and smelt Her smell, but my memory serves me well, still after All the alcohol, after all the toxic substances I have consumed, my memory of Her is still my Special place. Time can never erase that. Self destruction cannot erase that kind of Purity I Felt.

I know in those passing Minutes and Hours I have spent some amazing Time with some amazing People, whether it has been 5 Minutes to 3 Days to 6 Years, I don't regret any of those Moments. They are all eternal.

Thank you All Eternally.

Goodnight.

Eternal Love,
Nicole Marie Halls.

Good Evening God/Goddess and All,

If I was to think about what I truly want, what my Heart wants, without fear of judgement and without fear of loss, it goes as following:

I want to have these Journals published and made into a book. I want to be an Artist, of some sort, in some manner. I want to Study and Help People move beyond their struggles if thats what they choose. I want to help People achieve their goals and to see their reactions and know that I have made an impact in this World. For this World is mighty and Beautiful and I want others to share in this Divine experience with me. I want to be a Mother, whether I must do that on my own I will. I want to Travel.

If I must use "I am" statements, All I got is this: I am a Woman that has immense Love to Share in this Life, this Gift I have been given. I ask of You, Spirit, to help me fulfil my Destiny.

I know I want a lot, I know that, I know there is more within me that is still hidden behind judgement and fear of loss, but it will come forth and I will rise out of the Darkness into the Light where we All belong.

Thank You.

Eternal Love,
Eternally Grateful,
Nicole Marie Halls.

Good Evening Goddess/God and All,

I have only slept perhaps 3.5 hours in the last two days. I have had waves of feelings as if I was withdrawing from prescription drugs, it really hasn't been a great feeling day for me today. But I am here and I am confused. I am finding it difficult to piece together my Life. I started writing a timeline of my Life last night and it just frustrated me and perplexed me. How can I not remember so much? I have Lived 32 years and I have snippets of memories of my Time here. My way of navigating Time is through People and the emotions I felt about certain situations. I don't remember the dates, years or times, I remember the smells, sensations, feelings, faces.

I was just having a shower and thinking about a Time when I was younger that I decided to take an overdose to get into a psych ward to see what I could learn, as if I was some scientist trying to learn new things. I went through with taking the overdose and getting into the psych ward but I couldn't tell you what I remembered or what happened while I was in there. Why would I have done that? I did struggle with grandiose ideas of being some super intellectual individual that wanted to learn new things and become a Psychiatrist and help people, but what have I done with myself? Like what am I doing?

I went for a walk before and thought about me being unique, which is the Truth, total Truth, we are All unique. I am no greater than any one of the individuals I saw down in the town of Alice Springs today. I am no better or different to anyone I have smiled at, talked to or walked passed today. So what is my purpose here in this Lifetime? What am I here to do? Because I cannot go back to Melbourne. The thought of talking with my Family, Friends or People I know back in Melbourne seems way to overwhelming today. Maybe thats because I am wired and can't sleep.

I want to tell a Story but I cannot find the words to articulate what I want to say. I know that I have experiences that may have some Value, but where do I begin, how do I construct anything when my memory fails me?

I don't want to complain here but I am so unsure as to where I am going and I am literally exhausted today and cannot think straight. I know it is about the journey, I know that intellectually but I am learning to take these experiences as the treasures here, and yes I want to face my fears and Dream big, but how big is big? What can one Woman Dream of? Do I dare to let myself Dream it? When there are so many choices in this Life where do I begin? This World can be incredibly overwhelming and today is one of those days for me. I don't want to stop or give up I just want to take a nap.

Am I lonely?

No, I have much to process.

I wanted to hide before, hide in the blackest, darkest, most silent place I could find before but I just couldn't think of where that would be. It was like I didn't want to exist but I didn't want to die at all, it was a strange sensation. I walked instead. I stumbled rather, I stumbled around thinking about what I can offer. What is my purpose? What am I here to express and experience? What am I here to give?

Eternally Grateful,
Eternal Love,
Nicole Marie Halls.

Good Evening Goddess/God and All,

I will start with Eternal Gratitude for my Existence and All the Blessings I have in abundance within my Life. To All my Family, Friends, Work Colleagues, Acquaintances, My Baby Cats, to you All, I Miss You, I Love You and I think about You daily. Thank You All for helping me grow up, Thanks for being in my Life and sharing your Time with me. I Hope You are All Happy, Safe, Well and Living in Peace.

I came up with some plans, because it seems that having back up plans for the things I can predict make me feel more secure. I cannot really predict anything, but I can imagine if things don't work out the way I do want and plan then I have an idea of what I could do in the chance of things not working out. So I am here in Alice Springs, trying very minimally to get a job, but putting things into place to get my passport.

So I should probably outline the actual plan prior to condemning it to fail, then I will outline my back up plans if All fails.

I am planning on getting my passport, saving money then driving up to Darwin. When in Darwin I shall save some more money, then when the Time is right I will sell "Pokie Girl the Wonder Car" and purchase a plane ticket to LA. I then intend to go to see the Ellen show and explore LA a bit. While All this is happening I wish to find a publisher to see if I can get these diaries published. If I cannot find one in LA I will head to New York. Now I will try my hardest to find someone to publish it but if that isn't the case then I will just hang out in New York a little, depending on money and the amount of Time I am allowed in the US I will just live as simply as I can.

So here goes the back up plans.

1. If Nikki won't sign and authorise my passport photo I will stay in Alice Springs for at least 1 year to get someone to be able to sign it. While staying here that year I will work, save money and live as simply as I can.

2. If I cannot get a Visa to enter America because of my criminal record I will still drive up to Darwin, explore the place then drive down to Queensland and start my Life there.

3. Again, if I cannot get a passport at All because of my criminal record I will just go to Darwin then Queensland and live some sort of Life I am unsure of yet.

4. If Nikki signs the photo and I get my passport and a Visa to America but I cannot find someone to publish my diary then I just have a little holiday and return to Australia with no real idea how I will continue to Live my Life.

5. I have no idea what I will do if I don't get to be an audience member on the Ellen show either.

I now know what I am capable of in terms of the working world, I know that I can actually do it. So maybe I would just become a nomad and travel around the Country. Or perhaps I would just become homeless, Live with other homeless peeps on the streets and share my Time with them.

I cannot see me having a Wife and Children to work a 9am-5pm job for, so I think becoming a nomad or homeless would probably be my best option.

I do not feel sad about these options because its All about attitude and if I was homeless but sharing my Time with other homeless peeps I would be Happy with that. I am sure they would Help me as much as I could Help them.

I have had the thought that I should get these diaries published, I am putting into words that I want these diaries published, and I am putting into action the intention to get myself to a place that may be able to help me get them published, so I am working with the God/Goddess to try and see what I can achieve.

I have thought about a couple of ways this may go, and I know that I literally cannot come up with All the possible outcomes of this situation but here are some situations I am preparing myself for.

1. I find publishers in America to at least read my diaries. No one wants to publish, for whatever reason, so I just try as many as I can until I have exhausted All my Time and money, or until I just cannot find anyone else to read it.

2. I am not prepared for the fact that these diary entries may hold some Wisdom or insight into something. I am not prepared to think that People want to hear my mixed up diary entries as if they have Value.

I know I have a story because I truly Believe that we All do. I Believe wholeheartedly that every persons story has Value and Insight and something to teach each other, I just don't know that if what I have written makes any sense at All.

I know enough about myself to know that I was put on this Earth to do something Creative and Inspiring, I just don't know what that is yet, hopefully in Time I will learn what that is and be Brave enough to share it with other Human Beings.

When I walk down the street here in Alice Springs, or Adelaide, or Melbourne, or really anywhere I go I wonder what everyone is thinking about. I Wonder what these People want to be, or what they already are and how they share their Love and genius with the World. I am so curious about other People that I sometimes lose sight of who I am and what I want to do. What do I have to share that is any different or more unique than anyone else? I share everything that everyone else has, I may be unique yes, but so is every single Human Being I walk past or say "Hello" to every day. I know not what to do with myself in this World. I always wanted to Help people, but how can I when I know not what I have to offer that may Help.

When I was in Melbourne I had decided for the first Time that I would dedicate myself to really start and finish this University course to become a Social Worker. I did some research and read some chapters from a Book Amy gave me about what it would be like to be a Social Worker and I really felt that I wanted what this course had to offer. I agreed that I wanted to fight for Human Rights, I feel that right now, more than anything. I feel like there is nothing else I could do in this World other than fight for Human Rights. I had prepared myself to do the oral presentations that had scared me out of every other course I had tried to start, I was working on ways to prepare myself for moments of truly not knowing things so I could become a Social Worker and help People. I was working so hard at preparing myself for this Journey to become a Social Worker, and now I know not what to do. There is nothing I am more Passionate about than wanting to see People thrive, to see People achieve a goal that they think they maybe couldn't do. I have experienced that feeling myself and it still blows my mind to think of being able to do something I really didn't Believe I could do. A simple yet Powerful example of that for me was finishing High School. I have the greatest Enter score ever, 58.40. I didn't get into one single University course I wanted to do, my Enter score was not high enough, but it's the best score because I actually got one. I could have gotten any single number as my Enter score and I would have been ecstatic, because I actually finished High School. Not every year was awful in my High School years but there were a few that felt dark and the other years are dedicated to the Love and Support of my Amazing Friends. I literally wouldn't have finished without them and I Thank them All Eternally for helping raise me into the Human Being I am today. I always thought I was "Dumb", and I am sure I learned that somewhere but it really shook my ability to perform at school, so it was a great achievement to have finished High School and get the Enter score I did. My point here is that even with the Love and Support of my Amazing, Beautiful Friends I still didn't think I would have been able to finish High School. My Friends couldn't take the exams, that was entirely on me, and somehow I passed and thats All that mattered to me. I really do know what it is like to want to give up, I have tried so many things and given up so quickly but I have also done some good things too in my short Life, so for that I am proud of myself. I know not what the future holds, I will just keep making back up plans for All the things that could go differently, but as it has gone lately things are going very smoothly and I am very Happy and have All that I need. I Miss All the People I Love deeply. I don't need for anything. I am rich beyond Belief. I have more than enough money. I have a Car and Tent so I have two roofs over my head. I have enough food, cooking facilities, showers, toilets, a pool, transportation, entertainment, People to converse with, alone time, Nature, a Library, no need for a watch or the Time and I have Memories of All the People I Care about and Love, and All the Animals that have shared my Life with me. I am literally the luckiest, richest Woman in the World. I know I have a lot more I could give I just hope I find my place to do that in Time. Thank You Kindly for Listening to me ramble my little Heart out.

Eternally Grateful,
Eternal Love,
Nicole Marie Halls.

Good Afternoon Goddess/God and All,

I am Grateful to be Alive. I am Grateful to have eaten and that I have All that I need with me now. I miss my Family, Friends and Baby Fluff Nuggets.

I went to the NT Reptile Centre yesterday and I Loved it. I held a bearded dragon, a blue tongue lizard and some sort of python. I want them All as pets please. And All the Beautiful Geckos, I want them! So Beautiful.

I was surprised with a phone call from a place I had dropped my resume into. A place called "The Rock Bar". I was excited. I worked four hours yesterday, serving alcohol, taking orders, cleaning. Everyone there was so Lovely and I felt like I could handle working there. Everything went ok and I felt good when I left there. The tasks that were part of the job were not difficult, I was capable of doing what was asked of me and the general tasks at hand but last night I became so drained. I was exhausted by 9:30 so I went to bed. When I woke up I felt as if I had drunk half of the alcohol that was at that bar. I was foggy in the head, still exhausted and I just had this overwhelming need to cry. I really didn't think I could be around alcohol or serve people alcohol. My Soul just wouldn't allow me to continue. The thought of continuing just brought me to tears, so I am no longer there. Once I had made the decision to tell Fiona I couldn't continue my whole body felt lighter and free. I didn't want to cry anymore and my energy returned. I really don't feel passionate about serving people alcohol, not after everything I have seen and experienced. Alcohol has been a major influence in my Life and it didn't align with my values. I would prefer to be jobless than feel that way.

I have come to realise that it is not because I am not capable of the tasks of the job, that part is easy, it is more to do with what my Heart and Soul can handle doing and giving.

My Heart and Soul are singing now that I had the Courage to walk away from something that I realised was serving no one, not myself, nor the employer. I managed to keep the negative self talk and blaming myself to a complete minimum when my focus changed from thinking that I need money to knowing that the actions for which I was getting the money were not in alignment with my values and goals as a Human Being. My overall experience of alcohol has been a depressing, frightening, life destroying one and I don't wish to be a part of that environment.

I met a Lovely Man named Mark today at Max Employment. He inspired me. I was feeling low and his Smile and our interaction was the highlight of my day. We talked a little about ourselves, but what inspired me the most was the fact he was waiting for some reading glasses to be sent to him and he wanted to get his teeth fixed so he could feel better about Himself so He could find employment. These things are so simple but essential in making a person feel good about themselves. And with Indigenous People it seems that it is harder for them to find a way to get to the point of getting a health check, an eye test or their teeth fixed. This Gentleman was positive towards me and I truly wish him the best. Thank You Mark for making my day that much Brighter.

Eternally Grateful,
Eternal Love,
Nicole Marie Halls.

Good Evening Goddess/God and All,

Its safe to say I was a massive people pleaser when it came to sex. I truly lost the truth in knowing that sex is not Love. I have allowed men to do things to me I never would of thought I would have allowed. The shame I have felt in relation to sex and my body has been so enormous and detrimental to my growth and development. Some men's ideas of pleasure seem distorted and really need to be questioned. When a Woman allows Herself to void Herself of Dignity and Value and Love something needs to change.

If I think about the sexual experiences I can actually remember, I know I was only in the moment to please the other person so they would like me. Literally in every moment I was trying to please the other person.

I was just reading an article about the difference between sex and love-making, and I literally have no desire to have sex like I have had ever again. Hence the year long vow of chastity. I cannot even think about making Love because I can only think of one person I would want that to be with but she is Married, so I choose not to think of Her in that way. There is no other woman I can think of or have met that I would want to think of making Love with.

I am so restless tonight and have so much on my mind I cannot seem to type quick enough.

I miss talking to People.

I feel like I have been listening for so long, and I Love hearing People's stories and getting to know them, that is one of my Passions. I am not sure if anything I have to say has Value because I simply write it down and forget about it. I generally never re-read any diary entries, I just allow the words to flow and I leave them behind. I have no idea whether anything I have ever written makes any sense. I have no concept as to how any of what I have said sounds. I have feelings about some of the things I write. Like I have a strange feeling I may be slightly obsessed with Sarah, and if this were ever to be published I would be embarrassed to think that she may find me utterly crazy. I am so Passionate about writing and self expression that I want these journals published, but truly what is in this content?

Maybe there is something entertaining or of value in the words I have written, I literally wouldn't know, but the feeling is too strong to dismiss any longer. For some reason I have had the idea to travel to the US to find someone to read what I have written, and I have walked away from everything to do that, so maybe, just maybe...

I have listened intently to as many People as I could in my Life, and they have shared with me their Dreams and Fears, their Shadow and their Light, and for that I am Eternally Grateful. I could ask for no greater Gift than that, for self expression and active listening are Gifts that we All deserve. I hope one day I find the ability to gather the words for my story.

I am 32 Years Old and my Time has been spent in relation to others. I do not recall dates and times, I recall People and Stories. I remember moments and smells, songs and meals. I must have something to say.

Goodnight All.

Eternally Grateful,
Eternal Love,
Nicole Marie Halls.

Good Afternoon Goddess/God and All,

I have struggled with mental health issues since I was around 14 years old. I was first diagnosed with depression at 14 and put on medication. At 18 I was diagnosed with borderline personality disorder. A few years after that I was diagnosed with bi-polar and over the years I have also received the diagnosis of psychosis. I have been on a variety of psychiatric medications for over 18 years and this year, 2018, only in the last 3 weeks I find myself medication free. It was always a goal of mine to be medication free I just never knew if it was possible. It seems that it is.

I just decided to isolate myself inside of anywhere I lived and chose to try and kill myself slowly. I remember this day I had these intrusive thoughts, I was thinking I was going to hurt someone, so I went into Footscray Mall, bought cigarettes, smoked as many as I could in a row then called the police. I was convinced I was going to do something wrong, I didn't know what or when or why, I just thought I was going to. When the Police and Ambulance came I just kept demanding them to arrest me, but they wouldn't. I became so frustrated that they wouldn't arrest me, I was telling them to take me off the street, I was a danger, I couldn't understand why they wouldn't listen to me. I don't know what happened after that, hopefully they sedated me, but I wasn't arrested or put in jail.

For so many years I have just been waiting to be arrested and jailed. I have been expecting it, and in writing All this down I still have that expectation within the back of my head. It doesn't scare me, I have expected it a long Time.

Another moment when living in Empire Street I was experiencing intrusive thoughts where I thought the Devil was talking to me again. This time the command was as simple as shaving off All my hair, and this was to show that I was admitting to society I had commit the sins that I had. For some reason society was to know exactly who I was and by the act of shaving off my hair I was admitting to All that I had sinned. The experiences go on and on, the intrusive thoughts go on and on, the mental illness ebbs and flows but it is consistently there, it exists. From the age of 18 to the age of 32 that was my Truth. That was my Darkness, my Shadow and it was utterly shameful and painful, but I survived, and for that I am Grateful.

When I think of the Light I think of many Happy moments. With Family, Friends, Animals and Strangers. But I cannot deny any longer the greatest Truth of All and that is of Sarah. This Woman changed my entire way of experiencing Love. We were Best Friends and she Loved me and Cared for me. I couldn't see that at the Time, as I was already haunted by insecurity and the inability to take on the idea I was Loveable. But now, with the solitude I am experiencing I am able to see with clarity that she Cared for me greatly. This Woman shared with me Her Home, She shared with me moments of Light and Dark and that means a lot to me. My most profoundly Happy moments were memories of Her, and through some of my Darkest moments those memories have inspired me to continue to Live. The Love I have for Her is part of my ultimate Truth. I admitted to two Human Beings my greatest, Darkest Truth, my Shadow and that was liberating, but I have never had the opportunity to express to Sarah my ultimate Truth. If this Woman were to ever read these words I would Truly be liberated of All that I have kept secret for so many years. All She needs to know is that She is greatly Loved, nothing more, nothing less, it's that simple. Thank You to every Human Being I have ever shared Time with, without You I would be nothing. To All Human Beings Alive, Our Value is Priceless, Our Love is Our greatest Gift and we need to share this as intensely as we can with as many Human Beings as We can. Thank You Kindly for listening,

Eternally Grateful,
Eternal Love,
Nicole Marie Halls.

Good Morning Goddess/God and All,

I felt like I forgot what I was here to do. And while my mission here on Earth is still not crystal clear in my consciousness, I have remembered that A Mental Health Revolution is necessary. I just watched a speech by Lady Gaga, and it was inspiring and I Thank Her for using Her position to inspire other Woman and Human Beings to use their Voice.

I have these memories of when I was younger, I had this crazy idea that if I pretended to be "Mentally Ill" and an "Addict" I would do what I could to get myself into a psychiatric ward, a detox and a rehab and do research from the inside. You see I wanted to be a Psychologist, like for as long as I can remember. Helping People has always been my passion, but I knew not how to go about it. And who was I helping if I had no experience of the conditions by which these People were suffering. So after not getting the Enter score high enough to get into Psychology at University I quit my first job as a Kitchen Hand and decided I would dedicate my Life to my addiction and crazy ideas. I was getting income from Centrelink so I still had money but I was completely aimless and goalless. Although it seemed I wanted a way in to study these places from the inside it became a self fulfilling prophecy. I had these ideas of helping by experiencing and by Believing that I was experiencing for a purpose unknown to anyone but myself I actually literally became Mentally Ill and an Addict.

While I do admit I had traumatic things happen to me throughout my Life there were moments of utter clarity where I had these what seem like crazy ideas now, to consciously take an overdose to get into a psychiatric ward. The best idea I had was to become a patient. From that perspective I could Learn much more.

Somehow over the years the lines blurred between my conscious decision to become a "Patient/Client" and real Mental Illness and Addiction becoming my identity. It seems so hard to explain now but it was clear to me in many moments the way I could Learn how to help People the most was to embody a role, to embody a diagnosis and try and see things from their perspective. Now maybe what I am writing now is All part of one of the many Mental Health diagnoses I have received, but at the Time I was living it, it was real, as real as anything I have ever experienced. It was my Truth and I Lived it to the best of my ability. I have made many mistakes along the way on this journey of discovery, many mistakes that have been lost between reality and delusions, but I know underneath it All I started out with the best intentions in my Heart. I am here now, in Alice Springs, decompressing from the Life I have lived over the past 14 years. The last 14 years have been the years of the majority of my Mental Health and Addiction Journey. Whether I chose this path or it was bestowed upon me I would never trade one moment for another reality. The People I have met along the way have made the Journey worth while. I have met Amazing, Inspiring, Funny, Beautiful, Uplifting Human Beings trying to navigate through Life, doing the best they could with what they had at every given moment. Without these People I wouldn't be who I am today.

When I was 23 I decided I wanted to go to Rehab, so I made that happen. I went to a program run by the Salvation Army called "The Basin". I was there around 4-5 months and I completed the whole program. I was very determined and I achieved my goal. I am very proud of those months. While at this program it became clear that I wanted to be an "Artist". I didn't know what this meant or involved, it just became my favourite thing to do. To express myself creatively. There were Art Therapy classes run throughout the entire Time I was there, I Loved it, it was my favourite thing to do. I locked myself away in my room and stayed there for hours thinking about ideas, drawing, writing, making and creating. I felt strong and light and as if I had found something that would be a way of expressing myself that I had never had before. It made me Happy. I know in My Heart that every one of Us has something of Value to say, We are creative Beings with the power to express ourselves, we have just lost the ability to Believe that we are Worthy of being listened to. We have lost our Voices to the pain and fear we have learnt over All the years. I don't know specifically what I have to say or if I will ever find the right medium to Truly express myself, but I know my Heart and Soul has the Passion and desire to find a means of expression.

I wanted to study Social Work to fight for Human Beings' Rights, our Birth Rights. I Believe nothing more Passionately than the need for Mental

Illness to be of the highest priority possible. Mental Health affects every single Human Being Alive. In some way, whether You we are aware of it or not, everyone, every single Human Being Alive right now is affected by Mental Health Issues. Whether it is a personal experience, an experience of a Loved one, a Friend, a Colleague, We are All connected, we are All closer than we think. Mental Health affects every level of society. From Children, to Teenagers, to Adults and every category in between. Mental Health Issues affect every single sub-category of Human that You would like to divide Us into. Any Human Being that has been labelled as "something", or categorised in some way, shape or form, is affected by Mental Health Issues. This division is creating Illness. Do We need these "categories" and "sub-categories" as Human Beings to create an Authentic Identity?

I am Thankful to Lady Gaga for sharing that speech she made, and to All other Human Beings sharing their stories as inspiration for others to use their Voices. I am remembering that Mental Health has been a massive part of my Life. I am a Woman finding Her Voice after fighting for over a decade with Mental Health and Addiction Issues. For a long time I struggled to realise that those labels were not entirely who I was. We are multi-dimensional Beings, and I have survived Mental Health and Addiction Issues. They are not entirely who I am, they were experiences that I have had and now I have found a way through them with management strategies and lifestyle changes.

When I was in DAS WEST in Footscray, a detox unit, I really embraced the Art Therapy, and one day I gave the staff a small picture I had coloured in, and on it I wrote, "From substance abuse, to building substance of character". I am still trying to build that substance of character every single day I am Gifted.

Thank You Kindly.
Eternally Grateful,
Eternal Love,
Nicole Maire Halls.

Good Afternoon God/Goddess and All,

I Wonder about boundaries. The Earth has Natural boundaries by the way of Hills and Mountains and things like that but we, Human Beings, divide the land with invisible lines and boundaries for what purpose? Perhaps I don't understand how rules and laws can change after you have crossed an invisible line that divides the Earth from one thing into another. My mind is incapable of understanding how this can work. When in Melbourne I would stare at the map of the World and Wonder why there was so much division. It is All Man made. I imagine that Man wants to own and conquer something that cannot be possessed. We have taken the need to have personal boundaries as Human Beings and placed them on the Earth. It literally makes no sense to me. If I own my feelings and thoughts and actions I gain power. I take responsibility for the behaviours I have chosen and make a conscious effort to be aware that other Human Beings have needs as well. By being aware of my needs I can become aware that everyone else has needs, and while I know now it is not my job to fulfil the needs of others I can still support them in their achieving their needs.

I cannot express the ideas in my head at this moment and it is frustrating me. Boundaries are essential in the development of healthy relationships. Finding your boundaries is a process and the development of the skills to use your Voice to articulate and express to others what your boundaries are is growth. I know that the idea of dying for the rights of other Human Beings seems Noble, I am sure many People have wanted to do this, but what if there was another way?

What if we could reclaim what is rightfully Ours? Because we give ourselves away each and every day to many different People, compromising who We are and what we stand for. If we could reclaim ourselves, reclaim our identities, reclaim our values and Beliefs. Our Heart knows who we are, its our minds that trick Us.

I cannot articulate what I want to say. This is annoying me deeply. Its like I see things as they could be, a different way, a different perspective but how can I share where I am coming from if the words escape me?How can

I judge whether what I am saying has Value? I feel as if everything I say makes no sense, but what if it did? Children need to learn about emotional health, it is essential in changing the World. Children need to be given enough space to develop their own awareness about who they are and I guarantee the World will change. The Children are our future and it is our responsibility to model for them positive Life choices. I cannot dictate what is right or wrong when raising Children, I am in no position to do that, but I know in my Heart that the Children of the World know more than we would like to admit. They are Pure Love, We are All Pure Love, they want Love to prevail, they know the way.

The greatest Gift I could ever give my Children would be to take Care of myself, stand up for myself and share the Love that we have within us, to every single Human Being, no matter the circumstance or story. There is Authentic Power in claiming your Birth Rights, they are bestowed upon Us All and we need to realise We are All worthy of their Power.

I must admit this has been one of the most frustrating diary entries I have ever tried to write. I have made no sense, I haven't been able to convey the message I wanted to and I still have more to say.

Please Lord and Lady help me find a way to express myself, for if I don't I may explode.

Thank You Kindly for listening to me dribble random words that make no sense.

I am Happy to say I have nothing left to write at this moment.

Eternally Grateful,
Eternal Love,
Nicole Marie Halls.

Dear Goddess/God and All,

The boundary of my skin is barely containing my shame. I have showered but the intensity is overwhelming, so much so it feels like I may have a heart attack. I have been trying as many strategies as I could today to help myself, and it has worked. When I went on a walk this afternoon I passed two ambulances, and usually in the state I am feeling that would be me in the ambulance experiencing a crisis, handcuffed and sedated as it has been. The screaming lights of the ambulance remind me of the agony I have endured, the self induced crisis after self induced crisis, moments where the intrusive thoughts became my reality. I haven't had a bad day, I have just been experiencing a heaviness of heart, moments where I am drenched in shame, a consuming guilt where Love doesn't exist. I remind myself that Love exists, I think of Her and I know that Love exists.

I am experiencing the eternal now in what has been labelled as Friday, if I am lucky to wake to experience the eternity of tomorrow it will be what I know it as Saturday. Saturday and Sunday are timeless days, Time ceases to matter. My phone is for music videos only, the clock is irrelevant, no one will call and I can exist with no expectation.

I am having lucid moments of awareness that I exist and We are All connected, I am enjoying these moments immensely, the power of connection is a necessary part of the Human experience.

Yesterday I went to the night markets in the Heart of Alice Springs. After enjoying the live Music and People watching I met these Lovely Aboriginal Men. First I met Daniel, then Lindsey, then Jo, Selwyn and Scotty. We sat on the grass and had a yarn for a while, what a Beautiful night I had. I was so elated and energetic last night, I was radiating Love.

I exist amongst such diverse Beauty, my Heart overflows with intense Love and I am beginning to Believe that I am a part of the We. For so long I Believed I didn't belong here, I thought I was invisible, but I am beginning to see that I am a part of this Eternal whole, this Us that creates Life and Love, and I Love it very much.

Thank You All. To my Family, my Friends, my Animal Children, to All the People I have met, will meet and the People I may never get to meet, We are All Beautiful, We are creatures of Love and Light and I am Eternally Grateful to be Alive. Thank You Goddess/God for All that I have experienced and may get to experience in the future.

Thank You Kindly.

Eternally Grateful,
Eternal Love,
Nicole Marie Halls.

Good Evening God/Goddess and All,

I am contemplating what I have been blessed with, the People I have known, the Family and Friends, All my Animal Children, my ex-partners, anyone I have been blessed to spend Time with. I have always experienced material abundance, I have had tens of thousands of dollars in my bank and nothing in my bank, and I have been rich throughout it All, I just Wonder where I go from here. How can I return the Love that I have been given? When experiencing the intense shame over the last few days, the intrusive thoughts to hurt myself have invaded my mind, but I Believe that if I hurt myself I would be hurting anyone that has cared about me, for we are All connected. I Wonder what I haven't experienced in Life? I am extremely curious to see where this All takes me, for I already feel like the richest Woman Alive. Thank You to All those People who Live within my Heart and Memory, you are All Precious.

Eternally Grateful,
Eternal Love,
Nicole Marie Halls.

Good Afternoon Goddess/God and All,

Movement is the essence of creation.

I am finding myself in a very foreign situation. I am sober, homeless, no Family or Friends that I am familiar with, minimal money, no psychiatric medication, no formal support system and I start a new job next week. My moods have been like waves, I am triggered by the slightest thing but I am managing to hold it together. I truly forget that I have and still am, I guess, struggling with Mental Health Issues. My own expectations of a moment where I just find myself "recovered" seems ridiculous when I think about it, but thats the kind of pressure I put myself under. I firstly forget that recovery is a life long process, and secondly I forget that I have had at least 5 different diagnoses within around 18 years.

I am managing to keep myself safe which is my top priority. The intrusive thoughts come, I cry and scream, but I manage to allow them to flow through me with no harm done. I just noticed that a lot of my coping strategies that I once used are only fleeting thoughts in my head, I feel as if I have found things more beneficial and healthy that I can turn too, which is an amazing feeling. I am in a completely unfamiliar place, with only myself to rely on, and it seems that I can be resourceful and achieve things when I'm set my mind to it. That awareness is an achievement within itself.

I want a moment of coherent expression, where I feel as if I have made some sense, and maybe, just maybe said something that holds value within the World. Most of my Art and Writing feels somewhat confusing, as if it makes no sense at all. And I am disappointed that I left my Art and Writings behind in Melbourne. They were expressions of my Soul, a part of me forever gone.

Independent: Not relying on others for support, care, or funds; self-supporting.

Self-Determination: The process by which a person controls their own life.

Self-Sufficient: Needing no outside help in satisfying one's basic needs. Emotionally and intellectually independent.

I was just reflecting, and I found myself thinking that being Loved by my Children would be a Beautiful by product of their creation. Seeing them Love themselves seems like it would be the most rewarding thing about being a Parent. If I could be a factor in teaching my own Children to find a Love for themselves that is so rarely seen now days, I would be the proudest Parent ever to exist. I offered to the Earth a moment of vulnerability tonight. In the darkness, alone, between the shadows and the sounds of imaginary predators, I offered my weakness of will. A part of me that needed to be acknowledged and now healed. Nature, in its essence is constant creation without judgement, it is always in motion, becoming more than it was with absolute dedication to the present moment. Nature holds space for me, it creates moments where I can challenge my Heart to be open to the Darkness I suppress.

In my becoming, this creative transformation within me, I notice I am grasping too tight to the past. I must make space in my consciousness, I must become aware of the need to integrate the People and experiences of my past. The parts of me unmentionable must become accepted and integrated so I can walk toward a place unknown, yet intuitively known as "The Most Beautiful Thing You Have Ever Seen". I have Dreamed of this place symbolically, I know it intimately, yet I have never experienced it. I am Grateful for the opportunity of this Life, for I know I will Live to see and know something so profound that one second of its Beauty will suffice.

Thank You Kindly.

Eternally Grateful,
Eternal Love,
Nicole Marie Halls.

Good Evening Goddess/God and All,

Some things seem as if they should stay unspoken
As if once uttered
The World may stop revolving.

Perhaps this limitless dialogue
I am engaged with
would cease.
If only
I would open my mouth
and speak.

Hear this
I proclaim
Shame had blinded my ability
to feel Love

My shadow dictates
My mass of cells
The blood shed
was only half the pain
The traces of disease lit up my eyes
While I sit partially naked
on the master's floor.

Here are my pieces
One for All of you
I cannot remember
In which moment of time
You belong

So I will stitch you All
to my beating Heart
So I can feel you with every breath

Don't forget to remember
I Love you All

I Love your shadows,
So please Love mine
I hope one day
we meet again
Until then
I will simply sing to you All.

Thank You Kindly,

Eternally Grateful,
Eternal Love,
Nicole Marie Halls.

Good Evening Goddess/God and All,

I am a Woman of simple words and simple expressions but my Heart and Spirit has depth.

I made a vow recently not to hurt myself. To stay Alive and stay safe. I Honour that vow by Honouring the memory of the Love and Trust Sarah shared with me, that purity is a Spiritual gift.

I want more than anything for this pain and agony to be transformed into a gift I can share with the World. I imagine if I face my fears I can accomplish any task gifted upon me.

I witnessed the Beauty of Nature and a reflection of my True Self today. A nymph shed Her exoskeleton right before my eyes. I was blessed to see this miracle take place. She was so fragile and delicate in Her constant movement, but after some struggles with Her legs she freed Herself into a new World. That experience blew my brain face away. Magnificent.

Eternally Grateful,
Eternal Love,
Nicole Marie Halls.

Dear Goddess/God and All,

I simply cannot comprehend the enormity of the situation we are All faced with. There is a crisis with the Healthcare system and the People in positions of "leadership" are blind to All meaning, they are consumed by greed and power, with what seems like no consideration for the People that make the Country function.

How can these Human Beings value money over Human Life? It literally makes no sense to me.

My Mother had the Dream of opening a free medical clinic, where All People were treated for free and with dignity and respect. I imagine that this would take an enormous amount of money, like an unimaginable amount of money to run, but I am sure that if someone was able to Dream of the idea in the beginning it would have to be possible. I am absolutely sure that a Free Universal Healthcare System would be possible, only because the Dream sounds impossible, but there in lies the Beautiful challenge. As I said, firstly if the idea is possible then I am sure there is a way of making it a reality. I am unsure of how I could contribute to this Dream but I imagine if I am passionate enough and value the idea enough then the Dream can become a reality.

I know wholeheartedly that I will meet the necessary People along the way that would help me make this Dream come true, I am sure of that, indeed.

My first thought would be about obtaining any sort of amount of money that would initiate a project like that. I cannot fathom a way as of yet to come close to the amount of money needed for something like that.

But I imagine Dreams start somewhere, and I have managed to accomplish things I never thought I would be able to attain.

I at least know that there would be professionals out in the World willing to donate their time and expertise for a willing cause like this, without financial gain. I am sure these People are motivated by something much greater than a desire for a pay check. Again, if the system worked well

People could be financially rewarded for their time, I am just thinking that I am sure there would be People that would donate their time and knowledge with the intention to raise the level of Health of the People.

Anyway, here is where I begin. This is an idea, something to work towards. I guess if I accomplish little there may be others after me that may take up the cause as well. I am sure with dedication, team work, passion and self-care this could be accomplished at some point in the history of Human Civilisation. The greatest Value in this entire existence is within each and every one of us. I believe that wholeheartedly.

Love is the most powerful energy in existence, and we must learn to appreciate the fact that it is Free. When we embrace this our Freedom becomes experienced and the World changes.

We All deserve this Freedom.

Eternally Grateful,
Eternal Love,
Nicole Marie Halls.

Dear Goddess/God and All,

I left behind years worth of artwork and writings, and I never knew their importance until I found myself in this position. Their value, irreplaceable. I cannot re create those moments of expression, I have grown beyond them. I never wanted to share my art or writing with anybody, it seemed too personal and I was always intensely vulnerable in moments of expression, but the thought of All those moments being destroyed hurts my Heart. My Art and Writing is literally an expression of Who I Am, an extension of my Soul, a part of me that I cannot replace nor recreate, priceless in fact. Where have those moments gone?

I am trying not to let one mistake or moment define my existence, for that would be an absolute limitation on my human experience, so I imagine I must let it go.

What if I don't have the words, images, photo's, or colour combinations to express the depth of my Love?

I made a vow to Honour the Love she shared with me and the Friendship that we had by not hurting myself, despite the onslaught of intrusive images and impulses, of which I have maintained quite well so far.

I will just keep trying, with All my effort to articulate my feelings through Art and Writing, then perhaps one day when I have the courage to share these expressions with Her, I hope she finds one element of something I have expressed that makes Her understand that she was Loved endlessly. We All deserve to know that we are Loved, that is the simplicity and complexity of Life, it is the meaning of the entire experience, to Love and be Loved, to share that Truth with your Partner, Family and Friends, in fact with strangers and animals alike. To give Love is to spread Freedom, for it is literally the only energy that is Free. Embrace and embody it's Power, for it can change us as individuals and it has the Power to change our World for the better. I have seen it, it's stunning to behold.

We are All irreplaceable.

Eternally Grateful,
Eternal Love,
Nicole Marie Halls.

Dear Goddess/God and All,

Happy Birthday to All Souls that find today to be the day they were born in any year of Time. I know not who you are, but I imagine if I had the opportunity we could celebrate together, so rejoice, however soft or loud at the fact you were born today. You were born with Birthrights, you are entitled to Love, so give yourself the opportunity to claim it, I promise you won't regret it. The battle in which we find ourselves has depth dimensions, layers of meaning unexplored, frozen within our Hearts, waiting to be chosen, so lets choose our choices. I have found the dimension of Safety and Trust, it was offered to me wholeheartedly many years ago, I have been there today, thank you kindly Sarah.

When All of my moments of expressions have become obsolete, Believe in the Children, for they are the Prophets of the future, that much I know.

Eternally Grateful,
Eternal Love,
Nicole Marie Halls.

Good Evening Goddess/God and All,

I prey for All to receive the message that We are All connected. It is the truth and the only path to Unity. To see the anger in someone else is to deny the anger within yourself, that rage is useful when given the opportunity to be transformed into the fuel that fires some grand creative Dream.

What Nicole, may I ask is your Dream? What do you see that no one else can see? Where is the need that can be fulfilled with the ideas floating within that skull of yours? And most importantly Nicole, do you have the courage to actualise this Dream? Can you face your fears? Can you embrace never knowing, for knowing is an impossibility here, is that something you are prepared for? Can you find satisfaction in any expression you have allowed into creation? Have you, Nicole, tried your hardest here, have you given every experience your All? Has every decision, every choice been something you would choose again? Would you die today and know wholeheartedly that the fight was worth fighting? Would you do it All again Nicole?

There is no hesitation as to whether I would walk this path again, I choose my choices. If I commend myself for one quality, I will acknowledge that I have tried my hardest in every situation I have found myself in. I believe I have given every ounce of strength humanly possible in any situation, at any given time. I have acknowledged and taken responsibility for the mistakes I have found myself to make. I have tried, so hard, to honour the pain without ending my life, something new to me, but deeply rewarding I must admit, and that is All I can do so far given the challenges I have faced.

What is my Dream?

I Dream of Love Uniting the World.

I Dream of Human Beings acknowledging each other. I Dream of a World where judgement is replaced by understanding, or the willingness to listen to another without reaction. I Dream of Forgiveness, on an individual level, starting with the Self, then I imagine it may spread to a place of

Global Forgiveness. I Dream of Healing the wounds of our inner child to allow the Children of the future the opportunities we may never have been given, for offering that kind of gift to another is a gift of Love for the Self and All of Humanity. I Dream of a World where the idea of death wasn't a scary idea, where We came to a place of appreciation for the time we shared, instead of thinking of All the pain and missed opportunities, where the Joy, Laughter and Stories overshadowed the intensity of the pain. I imagine if We find it within ourselves, this Belief, that we have tried All we could, pushed our own limits, Loved with every inch of our Being, that the pain and fear associated with death may become that little less intrusive, a little less controlling. I am deeply appreciative of the gift of life today. I truly never thought I would have made it to this age, 32, whatever that means anyway. I have come to realise I have played roles I never thought I would play, I made it to this day, where I can see, a little clearer than before, that Life is a gift, and I am not finished with it yet. I am finding within me the strength to Believe that there are roles within me that I have yet to play, that I want to play and will endeavour to empower myself to the point of creation. To every Family member, to every Friend, to every Partner, to every Human Being that has been a part of my Life, for long or for short, that has offered me a reflection of myself and the opportunity of Love and Growth, I offer you Gratitude and Love and the enjoyment of the Time we shared together. To the Woman I Adore, who offered me Truth in every expression and the Greatest material Gift I imagine to ever be given, a toilet roll holder from the High School toilets, I am Eternally Grateful for the Gift of your Time. I Love You Endlessly. Eternally Grateful,

Eternal Love,
Nicole Marie Halls.

Happy New Year to All of Creation,

There is a slightly unsettling feeling within me at this point in time. I am caught in a moment of reflection that is causing me deep confusion. Perhaps it could be the ego trying to teach me something profound, or perhaps it could be simplicity awakening within my consciousness, either way, I am confused. I have counted my Tattoos, and come to find that they mostly speak of Darkness. What am I trying to say here? What am I going to do with the space that remains when All the identification roles I have played become obsolete? Who am I? What do I do with myself? Is this doubt part of the process? I remember moments, scattered moments, sounds and smells and photo's and songs, I remember Her smile, I remember pain and pleasure, but what of expression? I don't know if I remember that. I don't recall talking very much, I don't remember hearing my own voice, I don't remember words or phrases, questions or interpretations, I don't remember Me. Who am I? What have I been doing with my Time? Does anyone know who I am? Do I create myself? If I do create myself, who do I want to be? How do you structure a transformation from a deep feeling of non existence to becoming some one? What motivates me now? What motivated me before? What, may I ask you, can Love create? What expression defines Love? For me, or any individual for that matter? Last night I performed a ritual to acknowledge one of the main parts of me, with the hope that who I am becoming is defined by Love. I know there is a loneliness that is apparent, a deep feeling of missing a connection, that is the Truth right now. I have built a Life, many times in fact, from places that I thought would consume me, but I maintained the strength in my legs, the core of me is blessed, so I find myself Alive and well, thankfully.

I am missing the symbolic meaning here, in this moment.

Live the Dream you've imagined it says, so what is that Dream Nicole? What have you imagined? Or more to the point what can your Heart imagine Nicole?

Eternally Grateful,
Eternal Love,
Nicole Marie Halls.

Good Morning Goddess, God and All,

I cannot sleep. When I cannot sleep I cannot Dream.

Sometimes I get confused, that is the simple Truth. I cannot distinguish between the facade or the Truth. Perhaps it seems obvious, but when I am in a certain state of feeling the messages become unclear and I am left feeling as if I have made a horrible mistake. These walls are strong, built solid, with a foundation unknown to me. I am sure you are showing me things that I cannot see at the time. What are these symbols of? Have I interpreted things in a manner in which I can process it? How do I organise the contents of my mind? The influx of information is intense, my senses are heightened and I am only new to this process, the new is also very uncomfortable. I must Forgive myself, I imagine Forgiveness is an essential concept here for All to learn. Is blame the opposite to Forgiveness? What are the feared responses we hide within ourselves that we think we may allow to happen if we let go of control?

Apparently the guilty get no sleep, so may I ask you Nicole what do you feel guilty about? What keeps plaguing your mind tonight?

Anger is the residual emotion I am trying to process now, but it wasn't the strongest emotion I experienced on Friday at work. Love motivated me to act as if I may have been "slightly" insane today. My goal before leaving this job is to touch the roof in that warehouse, preferably by jumping, which was completely unsuccessful today, but I imagine if I just keep trying I can attain that goal.

When I found my Wounded Inner Child I was surprised. I never thought I would see Her again. I imagine I found Her when I was strong enough to confront Her pain. I imagine that the reflection in my eyes was soothing and safe rather than frightening and cold. That took strength to find that place, where I felt comfortable enough for a Child that hurt to witness my Soul. In reflection I was able to offer Her a quality I never believed I was able to find, safety. Safety is essential to healing and growth, it offers the Body, Mind and Soul a place to experience space and space offers opportunities for growth.

When I was confronted with an instant Life or Death situation and coming to terms with Death seemed the only option, it opened a space for something new to emerge. Only upon waking does Life seem new, fresh, different some how. Meaning opens up and you can find it in the most Beautiful places, the strange places, the places no one looks, the Darkness, the neediness, the parts of you that you wish you could purge without feeling it first, the violence, the madness, the pain, All the unspeakable Truth that is buried between You and Me. This new Life isn't instant and it isn't enormous, at first anyway, One must prepare for the enormity of Love, One must inhale the tiniest of moments and become aware that Love is possible, Love exists. When you know something as Profound as Love exists, the madness of your search to express it begins. I guarantee this madness will make you Smile.

When I think of Happiness I think of moments IN time. A moment IN time has feelings, it has depths, it has textures and noises and smells and People. Moments IN time share connections, experiences, stories, smiles, hugs, gratitude and curiosity. Happiness has flavours that you can feel as well as taste, it is authentic expression without fear of judgement, it creates rather than destroys, it is a paradox and a moment of insight, Happiness is learning that Unconditional Love exists. It seems we have been too fearful to look it in the Eyes, it is Our Children, Our Own Inner Child and the Life of the Children We Create.

I imagine We are angry, angry with the pain, angry with what the pain represents, angry at the loss of our potential, angry at the loss of our voices, angry at the misunderstanding as to why we weren't loved wholeheartedly. I imagine we are angry with the inability to express the pain, angry at each other for controlling each others lives, angry at ourselves for allowing others to control our lives, angry at the guilt, angry at the shame, angry at the judgements and angry to the point of blame. I imagine anger to be pain amplified, pain constricted and distorted, pain unexpressed, pain withheld from the light of release. Pain and Anger are simply forces that have yet to be created into something Beautiful, something Worth sharing, something We can All Learn from, something We Can Love.

It is IMPOSSIBLE for Love to be stolen from You. If you can purify your Heart, even the tiniest bit, I Guarantee you will be the richest Human Being Alive. The greatest knowledge that I have encountered is that Safety is internal and Love can be stored there without fear of loss or ruin.

Sarah, I spoke your name, finally. I heard myself say your name and I smiled. I felt your radiant smile, and I smelt your essence. You remembered me, Thank You. I ask of You to witness me, I ask of You to hear me, I ask of You to choose to know me, I ask of You nothing more.

Eternally Grateful,
Eternal Love,
Nicole Marie Halls.

Good Morning Goddess/God and All,

I imagine my place of anger to be deep. I imagine this place of anger to be dark, without air, a barren place where mere existence is questionable. I imagine this anger to be consuming, to be blinding to the Truth. I imagine this anger to be powerful, a place where Love exists but takes millions of moments to find. I imagine patience can be developed within this stormy anger, I imagine that Dreams are haunted and the colour Green exists outside of me, not within. I imagine this anger feels as if All you could Create becomes drenched in Shame, and Life itself is reduced to a dollar value, I chose not to imagine anger anymore.

Here's something I know: Knowing, for me, is the simple experience of Time. It is a moment in Time when you feel the depths of someone's Darkness but you See the enormity of their Courage. In One moment Life can be Eternal and soaked in meaning, so Beautiful your existence becomes Known and Experienced, You find your Power. These moments in Time deserve Safety, they deserve the Freedom of Choice. We deserve to Know that our Birthrights are possible to actualise and that We are Worthy of the Glory of their manifestation. Each of my moments so far have Names and Faces, these moments have Stories and Dreams, Creative potential that when Discovered can Illuminate the Darkness for at least One individual in One moment of their Time.

I have come to see that Our Time is the Value of Our Existence. Our Time, when owned, becomes the Freedom We have Dreamed of, it allows for Peace to Flourish and Unconditional Love to Be.

Eternally Grateful For Your Time,
Eternal Love,
Nicole Marie Halls.

Dear Goddess/God Within Us All,

I don't want this to be the last thing I write. I want People to know how I feel, but I don't want this to be the last of my expressions. In this moment I am trying to accept the fact I am going to Die, cease to Exist. Hear this: I don't want to Die. I want to Know and be Known. That seems like the most Profound thing I have said in a long Time.

I existed as a reflection of All of Us, and what I have found in my Existence is Love. Profound Love. Deep Love, a Love that Sustains and Creates, a Love that Cares and is Thoughtful. Passionate Love, Soft Love, Kind Love, Funny Love, Creative Love.

I've experienced Fearful Love, Violent Love, Controlled Love, and Unconscious Love but that is not the Love that remains in my Heart, that Feels like Confused Love, Misunderstood Love, Judged Love, Love that is drenched in Pain, the only Love we may have Known.

I See and Feel the Enormity of Strength each Human Being contains, that strength can be Transformed into the Greatest Love Of All, Self-Love. We All Deserve this Love, it is Our Birthright.

My Journey has come to an End, although I know that the Depth of Self-Love has yet to be expressed. Self-Love in Essence is Equality.

Thank You Kindly for Sharing Your Time with Me.

Eternally Grateful,
Eternal Love,
I Love Us All,
Nicole Marie Halls.

Good Morning Goddess/God and All,

I find Myself in a Moment of confusion, a Moment where a choice point is forming and I am wanting too much information, I am not allowing the process to flow. What of the things I have said? I have read back some entries this Morning and I find a part of Me that is different to Who I Am Now. I feel as if I am judging Myself, which is not Helpful at All. This Journey is a process, a flowing through of Idea's, Moments that can be described as Time. If I find Myself holding on to One Idea of Myself, "Control", I lose the ability to Grow and Evolve. If My mere survival is where All My attention lies, possibilities become obsolete, Growth ceases and Love cannot develop. If Homeostasis, balance, is the goal, then I must Learn to let go of All that causes Emotional reactions. I am a Human Being. Everyone I meet are Human Beings. I exist. Others exist, so We exist together. I am no Greater or Less than anyone else, We All have the same potential. Our bodies consist of the same systems. We All have brains and We All experience Consciousness. We All grew within Our Mother's Body. We All have Parents. We were All created by a Woman's Egg and a Man's Sperm. We All Urinate. We All Defecate. The processes in which Our Bodies function are the Same. We All have Skin. We All are Ignorant. We are All Informed. We All Care. We All Fear. We are All Worthy. We All Belong. We All make Choices. We All Love. We are All Connected. We All have the Ability to Express Ourselves. We All question the Meaning of Life. We All have Friends. We All experience Morning. We All experience Night. We All have organs. We All have a Voice. We All have Feelings. We All have Emotions. We All have Blood. We All have Bones. We All have Genitals. We All have Senses. We All experience the Breath. We All experience Joy. We All experience Pain. We All have Needs. We All have Desires. We All have consumed Food. We All have consumed Water.

Good Morning Goddess/God and All,

Yesterday I was a part of an Army. We sang songs of Love and Freedom and We walked in Unison to the Heartbeat of Truth. Love is Our Grand Uniting factor and We are All Soldiers raising Our Voices against this system of Oppression. I, Nicole Marie Halls, was a part of this and I am Eternally Grateful for that experience. We Remember and Acknowledge, We Sit and Stand in Recognition of the Human Beings that walked on this Earth, that left Us with Memories of Love and Joy, parts of Them that Become parts of Us, Change can Unite Us, I can Feel it.

Good Morning Goddess/God and All,

I write with Gratitude this Morning. I must thank the People for Sharing with Me their Time, for without You I could not do what I do. Thank You to the Energy that is absolute Female Energy, the strength of this energy within my body is enormous, some days I feel as if I could explode and cease to exist. Thank You to the energy that is entirely Male, I am trying my hardest to embody you with the grace and respect that this energy deserves. If I can find a moment to Align myself with these energies, I will.

Affirmations:

Words chosen thoughtfully, with grace and respect reflect moments of authentic expression that have the power to guide action and growth.

I have come to realise I have a voice. I acknowledge that today, in this moment. I must be aware of ego identification here and in every endeavour from this moment onwards. If I attach even slightly to my ego I could fall into something deep, something that reflects a part of the human condition that supports the destruction of our civilisation, something I do not want to actualise. I want my voice to be a beacon of hope, something powerful to All, a noise that sings of the beauty and magnificence of the world and the people who belong here. I have been influenced by many voices, but the voice that sustains me, the voice that helps me embody empowerment and strength is Hers, it is Love.

It seems that I can write.

When I marched with strangers I felt safe, I felt as if I belonged in the midst of no one I knew. I recognised the feeling though. I recognised that I had a voice. I heard myself raise my voice in protest for the most meaningful thing I believe in: Love. I was not alone. I have never been alone. We walked in Unison chanting. I learnt a lesson in Power that day and I am grateful to All who shared those moments in the Sun with Me. I walked away from ego identification, I walked away from a Power that has systematically destroyed Human Lives, I walked away and I am proud of that.

I ask the Goddess/God and All to test me, hear my call to be tested, and when I fall, as we All have done, and rise again like the Phoenix, may my strength be of this eternal now. May my strength be in the experience of exchange, when I receive help from You, and You from Me. May the strength of Love be My only Power, and may I realise and actualise this gift in hope that One and All of Us can feel freely the enormity, the magnitude of this blessing, Life.

Thank You Kindly,

Eternally Grateful,
Eternal Love,
Nicole Marie Halls

Good Morning Goddess/God and All,

This Morning I seek to express myself from My Imagination, a place of Wonder and Creation, a place of Possibilities and Vulnerability that deserves expression. I offer, with Unconditional Love, each Word to those I Care for. I dedicate My Time to Our Children, You are the Prophets of this World, Love is Your Power, so I dare You to use it.

Affirmation: Colours are genderless, your breath is your birthright, and fear is the fuel for change.

Good Afternoon Goddess/God and All,

I am experiencing these feelings of wanting to return to what I know. I know how to navigate those plains of existence, the comfort of knowing is strong. I imagine this is a major choice point, where I could return to All I know, with a few experiences of the unknown, but the majority of my Life being a succession of moments filled with familiarity until I literally lose my ability to think and function for myself. In these moments my mind is clouded from any idea of anything I want to achieve, if I really know what that is to begin with. I don't feel scared, I feel exhausted. I feel like I have so much to give and no means to pursue this giving. I am screaming on the inside, well in fact I have just been screaming out loud lately, so much so I cannot talk properly. I Miss so many People, and I am trying to come to terms with letting everyone go. I am trying to experience the emotions that I have kept suppressed for so many years and move forward with Life. I have no idea where most of my Life has gone, and it is hard to build a concept of self when there is little to reference from past experiences. The moments of Love that I recall are grand and profound, I imagine they aren't always completely accurate in details but the sentiment and some of the picture is there, and I can't Thank each and every one of You for the experience of your Time.

Good Afternoon Goddess/God and All,

In All honesty I am starving here. I have eaten lunch but this hunger is deep and there is a void that needs to be filled. I imagine it to be something to do with my voice, or a lack of expression over the years. I imagine myself not to be the only one starving out there. I imagine myself to be one of many. But what do I have to say? And who will listen? How can I adequately express myself? Does anyone want to hear what I have to say? And in that exchange of acknowledgment, what of that? I am feeling overwhelmed and I want to cry right now. What am I crying for? I am safe in this moment, my choices seem limited because I am confused about how to spend my time right now. I have listened and watched for a long time now, and when I heard my own voice the other day, chanting in the crowd, I couldn't recognise it. It was an experience of something new, something so foreign and uncomfortable I simply wanted to hide by myself. I am writing, as simply as possible in this moment the feelings that I have. Sometimes I hope for wisdom to come to me so when I say something it has meaning, but today I am simply expressing myself. What of All the questions I have asked? What of All the questions that go unasked in general? What happens to the thoughts that don't become ideas and creations? Where do they go? Such profound wisdom lost. What if something I have thought could positively influence another to have an idea and then something useful is created? Of these moments lost we stay stagnant in fear and grief. Evolution requires courage. This World is so Magical even now with War and Hate, but I simply imagine with small doses of courage how much more beautiful it could become. From a place of contemplation and not of grandeur, what Guardians, is my role? How do I embody the strengths required to pursue the thoughts within my mind? I have had many ideas for Art projects, and only a few have been written down, and even fewer have been finished and actualised. Sometimes I feel lonely when I am alone, and in this moment it seems that I am lonely. When alone and lonely no one hears me, not even myself.

Affirmation: A thought actualised holds the power of creation.

Eternally Grateful,
Eternal Love,
Nicole Marie Halls

Good Evening Goddess/God and All,

It seems precious, these expressions we Share. I observed random notes of Love today, only to fight back tears of a longing I long to dismantle. I imagine Love to be grand enough that mourning transforms into Humans rejoicing, enjoying the memories shared, the celebration of souls colliding, a trustful embrace, momentary bliss, I still Wonder about You Sarah. With colour and joy the darkness transmuted from a substance that destroys, to a fire of creation, embodied, timeless, alone and free.

I doubt the symbols within my dreams today, I doubt the sound of my own voice. I walk away from an empty crowded room only to find a longing for something I am looking for outside of myself, something random and absurd, the meaning of meaning itself.

I cannot pretend to know many things, I only know that the nothingness I know something about is a contradiction that no longer causes confusion, it ebbs and flows like my ability to form coherent sentences. My inability to apply make up is an issue for me these days, it seems that my creativity knows no way of knowing just how to apply the perfect shade of blue.

Affirmation: Healing is a path to an alignment of Mind, Body, Soul and Spirit, We All have the Power of this path of transformation. We are the Goddess/God We seek.

Eternally Grateful,
Eternal Love,
Nicole Marie Halls

Good Afternoon Goddess/God and All,

When I was in the Northern Territory I witnessed People, Human Beings of Aboriginal descent, starving for Culture, filling in their time with the destruction of themselves. I couldn't tell You how many times I was approached to purchase drugs or alcohol for them, simply as I was walking into a shop. I chose every time to deny them their offers. They would reward me they said, with money, but their existence is worthy of more than a white woman buying them the means of daily destruction. I spoke to these People, I asked their names and we shared a brief moment in time, so many times. I want to know their Culture, I want to breathe their air and hear their stories. A culture doesn't live for over 60,000 years without destruction, for no apparent reason. These Human Beings cared for this land upon which we stand, they cared for each other until each and every member could care for themselves. Family was sacred and abundant, a primary source of pride and power. I sensed and smelt their destruction on their breathes, a violent mix of liquor and cigarettes, a union, the grand means of extermination, afforded to them from mostly Government money.

Their Art, oh the Beauty. I find Aboriginal Art to be complex and simple at the same time. A means of expression inherent in what I have seen of their culture, a way in which their stories become the children's inheritance. They are maps and movies, songs of ancestors and a way to define who they are at present and how the land sustains them. A raw nakedness of expression, passionate and forgiving, if only the system would hear their stolen cries, if ears weren't deaf to the howls of innocence, and my skin colour wasn't a reminder that People before me raped their souls with war, shame and devastation. How does the Healing process begin and continue for these Aboriginal People? How does my existence, as a white Woman, with the Dreams and Hope to carry an Aboriginal Child within Me, find expression one day? I find myself acknowledging that my cultural background is of Aboriginal and Torres Straight Islander descent on forms and questionnaires, but I don't have the honour of belonging to a specific mob. I find their Culture to be something I want to be a part of, their stories, the depths of their passions, a history marred by shame.

I ask, can I have a chance please? Can I, a Human Being, with Respect in My Heart share your Land and Culture please? Can I be given that opportunity please?

Thank You Kindly.

Eternally Grateful,
Eternal Love,
Nicole Marie Halls.

Good Evening Goddess/God and All,

Here is a moment, a thought caught in a tunnel of doubt. Suspicion and turmoil boiling beneath my skin. Scathing comparisons and a major feeling of anger. What am I doing? There are so many things happening in front of me, beside me, next to me, between light and shadows I cannot remember my name. I am confused and in need of this neediness to dissipate. What if this arrogance feeds my ego and I become something my values cannot value. What happens when these moments of confusion are driven by an anger of wanting to "know" the Truth. What happens if I cannot embody the Goddess, what if.....? So much information, it seems impossible to find a way to maintain equilibrium right now, help me Lady and Lord, help me in my search for the precise moment where something makes sense. Discipline and Truth, what do I have to share? Where are the insights Goddess/God, where is the wisdom of the time I have spent somewhere unknown to me? Where am I now anyway? I am in a place where identity exists in a fleeting moment, the breeze caressing my name upon my sense of hearing, and the birds continue to talk a language I cannot yet decipher. Is this empowerment, this power I could possess meant to build my strength to a point where I am alone? I struggle with Human interaction at times and I have been pushing myself beyond the threshold of comfort, so in this discomfort where do I find solace? Water I imagine, water.

I am known now only by You, only by the Goddess/God, because I have lost All sense of identity. I have been in bed All day touching myself, trying to embody the Goddess, only to find this doubt. In seeking pleasure I have found some pain, and I still don't know the goals of this enormous experiment. I am unsure of the simplicity that is required of me, walk with me momentarily so I can feel again what it is like to know myself, if only for a minute.

I surrender to the fact that I know nothing, but deep in this expression there might just be some fear. I ask of my Guardians to help me transform the pain and fear into a fuel grand enough that my expressions become known to at least ten other people within this lifetime. I don't want to be famous, I don't want to be rich, I want to be a Woman of Value, a Woman that shares the stage with others in collaboration and find strength in the places we have been afraid to shed light on.

Here is another moment, an expression of passion, a brief moment where my digestive system passes wind and I cannot help but inhale the stench. Here is the last moment on offer today, here I am Body, Mind, Soul and Spirit, in need of authenticity, in need of my own embrace, for I have a fear that the embrace I hope for will never be attained. I surrender myself to that fear, take it from me please. I have done my best in symbolically destroying the thread, that connection that I held so dear, a connection that helped me grow, so where to now? What part of the unknown can I know momentarily today? I have had glimpses of myself today, parts of me that shed light on the fact that I simply care, and for that I am proud. Go forth Nicole and bathe in the warmth that is the water of Life, be naked and hear the sounds of doves flying through the sky, this stream of consciousness has flown "My Sweet".

Affirmation: Love never dies, it transforms us, never to be what we were, only to be what we are innately, Light.

Eternally Grateful,
Eternal Love,
Nicole Marie Halls

Good Morning Goddess/God and All,

I write to You concerning information that has yet to be completely processed, so here I go. On the 19th of October, 2018, I drove from my Home in Melbourne, leaving behind All that I knew, All that I had built up until that day. I had a job, cats, family, friends, a car, the ability to vote, I could cook for myself, clean and maintain life as I knew I should have by a society that dictates how I should live. I attained that, I attained societies ideal living situation, minus a Wife/Partner or Children. So here is what it is symbolic of, my Death. I left everything as it was, I walked away from a fridge that was running, food that could have been eaten, bills that needed to be paid and a Life I was still preparing to Live. I had the goal to pursue further study, to become a Social Worker, to gain an education and further my opportunities and to contribute to the World, but that All changed. I admit, I smoked pot the day before I left, but when I drove that car heading towards Adelaide, away from my Life, I had made that decision. My mind was racing, as if thoughts were messengers, racing around and pushing me towards something completely unknown, something strange and new, towards parts of me I never knew.

From another's perspective, I had gone missing, and symbolically I had killed myself, I had commit suicide and ended the life I knew and could handle for a place of darkness, away from everyone I Loved.

I made no contact until I was literally classed as a "missing person's". I could not face the questions and was still unsure of my reasons. I am still unsure of the reasons completely, but All I know is that everything has changed. How could it not? My identity is fluid, in motion, a frequency that finds moments of clarity and moments of static. I want to begin to understand where I have been, for where I am going needs an element of stability, moments of recognition that can ground me in the present.

I have noticed that my Energy is quite intense today, I am opening myself to the Goddess, and it seems Her power is powerful. I have broken All threads between People I thought I needed to survive, only to find that my power of survival has been present in All the decisions I have made up until this point. People have offered me guidance and support, but it has been my choice to accept it and learn what I have needed to learn. I offer Thanks to those Human Beings and Myself.

Today has been a day of mourning, a day where old patterns emerge, become acknowledged and return to a place in my unconscious that stores things I may need later. But I have noticed many things today, one of the hardest things to let go of are Friends, my Friends I had in High School, so many memories there, precious moments with People I know little about now.

I choose Love to be my SuperPower, Kindness as my Weapon and Peace as the goal.

I am sure an Army of Lovers is Humanly possible, I wouldn't be granted the gift of the idea if it weren't possible.

I am an
Inhalation and exhalation,
A Heartbeat,
A process of digestion,
Moments of Wonder
And the seer of sights.
I am blood flowing,
Messages in transit,
Momentary clarity
And questions,
Just like You.
I have a name
But I am beyond Her identity,
I am a concept,
A philosophy,
Values and courage.
I am strength and capabilities,
I am Water
Movement

And Sex.
A World,
Layered with meanings.
The surface,
Superficial
Secure and safe.
I am the unknown,
Lost between
your knowledge and mine.
I am sweet, sour and salty,
A divided unity,
Blessed with Power
And instructions on how to use it,
Mostly though,
I am Human like All of You.
Beautiful pain,
Sacred and timeless,
I am the Eternal Now,
Evolving towards oblivion.

Thank You Kindly.

Eternally Grateful,
Eternal Love,
Nicole Marie Halls.

Good Evening Goddess/God and All,

Peace does not discriminate, it is a Universal Truth, attainable to All.

Eternally Grateful,
Eternal Love,
Nicole Marie Halls

To All on this Journey We call Life,

Love can only Unite Us. Our Freedom is found in the simplicity of experiencing each other's Truth. When We Know Ourselves, We come to find We know each other.

Our Value is in realising that Each and Every Life is irreplaceable, despite the doubt.

We Will find Trust, and it Will anchor Us; One moment Shared, in the name of Love contains the Power of Creation, it contains Life.

Beauty is a reflection, moments of awareness, authentic self-expression;

Beauty has names, stories, faces, a Smile; We are Beauty.

Our Eyes; Connection; Depth; Love.

That my Friend's is Power.

In the moment of acknowledgment We Know We Exist, and when We Exist the Fear becomes the fuel for Creation, and Creation is the Eternal Now.

That is My Truth.

Eternally Grateful,
Eternal Love,
Nicole Marie Halls.

Good Morning Goddess/God and All,

I have come to realise that the challenge available to me is not in the People that agree with me, but in the one's who's views differ from mine. I must find the strength to walk authentically, strong and determined in the knowledge that this idea is grounded in Love. I imagine that my stance may lead to difficult places, places of pain, anger, questions of doubt and moments of intense challenge. Is your foundation strong enough Nicole? Do your values give you the strength to move forward? Build a team of support and a network of friends. Find yourself in moments of reflection and know that all the tools necessary for this game are within your grasp. You are a warrior, you need to know that Nicole. You have proven your trustworthiness by the succession of choices throughout your life. Each choice, no matter what your judgement, has led you to this point, and this point will lead you to a position where power will become your responsibility, just know that you can handle the responsibility, it is your birth right, and from here you can only keep rising.

Human Rights are fundamental as building blocks for a foundation on the path to self determination. Change is possible, but it takes time, and management, self care and support.

Last night I yelled several times, "I Love You Nicole Marie Halls", it was odd but ultimately an enjoyable experience. The new is uncomfortable to begin with, it takes courage to feel your Heart racing as if it will suddenly burst out your chest, but to continue on, that's the part that becomes beauty, and We are All Beautiful, there is no doubt there.

Here I am unashamed, finally, of the body that inhabited and embodied shame for hundreds of thousands of moments within this short life. Here I am with a question, or two, but here I am sober, not under the influence of drugs or alcohol, completely capable of making decisions, willingly accepting a mental health assessment, mostly complying with police but simply naked. I had reached a moment of unexplored freedom, a moment where my heart rate was barely raised, my thoughts felt ordered and my conviction strong. "Give me a fine, please", I pleaded with the officer, for the amount this ticket is worth is nothing in comparison to the value I will find in the expression of this memory one day. I will plead ignorance until the truth in authenticity has become law, it is my birth right to understand the ways of this world I inhabit.

Spiritual growth and evolution of consciousness are a motivation for these expressions, if one sentence is relatable to another, then that connection is priceless. If one experience of mine is the fuel for a minor change or new experience for another, beautiful, I have achieved a connection that is a reward greater than anything else I can imagine.

I Love the sunlight but I also Love the warmth of the darkness when I am naked and writing. I Love the sensation of expression as a form of masturbation, my nakedness caressing words as they flow through me and out of me as I become wet with anticipation for the climax of the next full stop. I stimulate myself as each idea forms and becomes the growth of my spirit, soaring between the self imposed darkness and the light of creation. I give birth freely and with pain, pleasure seeking to inform me that life is a balancing act, a game of effort and love, each of us players, actors, muses, subjects worthy of our creation, worthy of the value of the human rights we know little about, worthy of self love. I am a Goddess and a God, an integrated individual seeking to expand and learn, with desires of passion and wounded places, deep within me, as I can see in you too. Look into my eyes, connect with me, I will not look away until you do, I will never look away again.

This process, visceral, an exchange between Me and Spirit, become seconds of bliss. When I talk I leave space for the emotion, I leave space for the process of change to demand a trace upon our brains, a fluctuation, deep ambivalence and the knowledge that I lactate faith. Let's communicate, shall we dance to the song of intimacy, the private taboo censored to the point of distortion. Let's communicate, how do you like to communicate? Let's communicate about communication, that sounds sexual to me, let's hear each other, once today, twice tomorrow and unconditionally on Saturday's. I simply want to know who you are, I have many questions, much time and my will is good, I hope that is enough. Your heat, the flames, I feel You, how do you feel me?

Good Morning Goddess/God and All,

I feel ancient today, as if I have lived several lives within the past four months alone. The amount of activity I have fit into such a short time equates to years of dismantling and processing. I am here today, exisiting with You in a moment never to be repeated in time. This day will only come once, this date is significant because it is unique like Us. My fullest potential is calling me to lay in bed and reflect upon time I have spent else where in this country, of another time and place, miles from here, unique like Me.

My addicted self has been sober over 100 days so far, and I am proud of Her. She came with me to the Northern Territory, broken, scattered and dismantled beyond recognition. Now she is flourishing towards goals of meaning and purpose, eating well and staying hydrated, enjoying pleasure and finding that being a Woman is an empowering place to Be.

I am feeling intense anger and confusion, and no strategy that I can think of would seem to calm the anger deep within. There are moments of wanting to lash out at something, but I will not do that, I will calmly navigate my way around the keyboard here. What of purpose? What is the purpose of All this? I see purpose being in the Beauty of the Evolution of the Human Spirit. I find meaning in places of simplicity, in the small, grand scale of the enormity and contradiction of time and experience. I want to scream, to shout and wail, loudly and painfully, with joy and elation. Where am I but in between? As the moment of creation arrives, it disappears and becomes a memory or a reflection if meaningful enough. What of this stream of consciousness of mine? Seriously?

Good Morning Goddess/God and All,

Here I am, in my nakedness, feeling Grateful for Life. Blown away, mesmerised, enchanted, in awe, but mostly Grateful. For from a moment of knowing you're alive there is only creation in front of You. There are only possibilities and challenges, lessons and joy, a feeling of safety that slowly unites with your worthiness.

Thank you for the air I breathe. Thank you for the water that cleanses me. Thank you for the warmth of my bed. Thank you for the convenience of the toilet near my room. Thank you for the choice of nourishing foods. Thank you for the flavour of my cup of tea. Thank you for the blessing of time. Thank you for the headache that indicates I need rest. Thank you for the house that I dwell in. Thank you for the incense that permeates my bedroom. Thank you for the People in my Life. Thank you for my past, for without those steps taken I wouldn't be here in this moment, safe, warm, filled with choices and opening my Heart to unconditional Love.

Who am I?

I am questioning the purpose of every movement, every breath and each thought that enters my head. For what reason would I have a bath? Why would I bother writing what I am thinking? Why should I get out of bed and eat? To cry or not to cry? If I smiled right now would it matter?

If I start from a place of breath, the simple inhalation and exhalation that is made possible by the miracle of Life.

What of my existence today? It seemed healing was the purpose of my day in bed, but what of the other tasks? Food, Water, toilet, shower, maybe thats self care in a moment this desperate for meaning. I am questioning everything. Questioning because nothing else seems to matter, in a place of aloneness one must find the strength to fight for Her Life. Do what you know Nicole, be kind and sweet to yourself, for you are worthy, despite the doubt.

Nicole Marie Halls, You are strong, undeniably so. You have made decisions that have impacted your life in magnificent ways. You have been fighting for a long time now, only to realise that All You have done has been made of your choices. You have made mistakes but taken full responsibility for them. You are caring for Yourself in ways you deserve to. You felt like screaming today, so you did, but no blood was shed, only tears. Your tears dried and you drove towards a destination unknown, with only the value within your Heart guiding you forward, be proud of that Nicole. Take each step forward knowing that You are a Goddess too. Your power is immense and the day you breathe your own light will be the day you Know that you are Worthy. You still doubt yourself Nicole, for moving forward with this level of power grants your dreams to come true, and you will see, soon enough how grand and beautiful your Dreams are.

You will embrace being alone, but you know you never will be entirely alone. Decisions will fall but you are a Warrior and you have the Strength, in your legs alone, to stand for the things you value. Your doubt will be painful, for responsibility like this is enormous, but so is your Love Nicole, Your Love is All encompassing, you will find Unconditional Love, you were born for this Nicole. Eternally Grateful,

Eternal Love,
Nicole Marie Halls

Good Evening Goddess/God and All,

I am contemplating writing a memoir but find myself judging my ability to grasp the concept of how a memoir is written. I am also taking myself on a journey of healing, through visualisation techniques, meditation, writing and creative pursuits. When looking at my "Shadow Self" today I saw Her depth, I revealed to myself the depth of who I was, who I am and who I could potentially become. That was a powerful and exciting moment, for the wisdom in those depths could just be amazing. There are diagrams and scattered notes, in random chaos and precise order of my thoughts and moments of expressions, all layered and dripping with meaning. I find it difficult to grasp one area of my life, analyse it and continue living. There is so much data that I could stay in bed for days and write, if thats all I was capable of doing. But there is more, there are moments of pleasure seeking, fantasies and imagination. Moments where the past reveals herself slowly, and moments of powerfully forceful realisations. If I could describe to you my experience I would use a mixture of words, sentences, textures, sounds, tastes and smells, for exploring consciousness can become messy, and it requires boundaries to become flexible and malleable, flowing and rigid, depending on the ideas at any given time. There is self imposed darkness, where the sight of myself in shadows becomes bearable, the air is easier to breathe and my internal light shines through on the page. Words become weapons against hidden angst and the desperation of parts of me untouched. Physical sensations become beacons of awareness that something is not healed, that a part of me is frozen, stagnant and in need of care. My choices require sweetness to manifest into actions and movement beyond this love affair with my mattress and pillows. I think I can move, but my judgements become louder, so loud in fact my nakedness falls short of leaving the bed I have made my home for today. Sleep cradles me, I am safe and healing, learning that dreams are messengers, angels guiding me and leading me towards hope. I am safe today.

Eternally Grateful,
Eternal Love,
Nicole Marie Halls

Good Evening Goddess/God and All,

In the adventures of my imagination I find myself reborn again. It seems that I have taken much note of the deaths of my life, with no real analysis of the births of myself. This birth seems clearer, as if I am granted access to parts of me that were unknown before. I am intimate with my shadow, she has become somewhat of a friend, a companion that I am still learning about. But who am I today? Who have I become? Or who am I becoming?

I am sensing more energy, an energy unknown to me, she makes noises that are unfamiliar and need to be expressed alone. I think it is a form of empowerment, a ritual to allow the body to manifest the new.

I wrote down the shadow parts of myself yesterday, only to realise there is a lot of space for the new parts of me to develop, so what of this? The Human mind, consciousness, is a creative well, or maybe even not, perhaps the Universe itself is a better used analogy, for space is expanding, and I am expanding with Her. These random expressions are only part of who I am, a scattering of words, ideas, phrases, sentences, mere minuscule moments of a world that I inhabit with profound wonder. I wonder, when someone cannot accept the terms of the present moment, where do they go? In which part of their memory do they hide? When accepting and living in the now requires the power to acknowledge change, in its entirety, the options of life become limited if denial is chosen.

I feel I haven't grasped the clarity of which I am hoping to attain one day within my lifetime, so when I express myself, I can be understood.

I have always had the desire to heal. The idea of healing has been a powerful influence within my life so far, and it still aligns with my value system to this day. I just wonder will I ever write one sentence that reflects the depths of my Heart?

The purpose of these Journal entries were to try and articulate my experience as often as possible, to find meaning and purpose in the cascade of emotions I have experienced over many days. This journal began as a way of finding a voice for myself, a dedicated way of healing the wounds of the past and express the beauty I have found along the way. In reading and reflecting on my past entries I have become overwhelmed at the words I have chosen and the structure in which they are formed, but I have found honesty amongst myself, a quality I didn't possess for too long. In thinking there was a purpose in publishing my writing, it seems safe to say that connection would be a massive motivation for the mere thought of allowing others into this space. I have experienced much, with the innate desire to help myself and fellow human spirits, so if one sentence, one utterance of sense is made here, and acknowledged by another, to the point where we share a common experience, I find solace in that. I find myself to have healed through the connection made possible by the experiences and journey I have taken in these short but passionate journal entries. In the reflection of these simple expressions I have found value in myself that seemed impossible at many points in my life, so a shared acknowledgment of the struggles and joys in life seems as if that has value within itself.

Within this journal I have demanded of myself entire honesty, a declaration that All parts of Me are shown and it has been my duty to heal and align them All. I may not have reached that alignment fully, but I know that I am surely on my way to finding more and more clarity as I am blessed with more days to live. I am a work in progress, a painting yet to be completed, art in waiting, ideas melting and a phoenix rising. What I find beautiful is that I am not alone on this journey, I have seen the beauty of kindness shared, love given, care taken and held tightly. I witness extensions of the heart often and it is overwhelming to think we don't see our value, we don't embody the greatest parts of ourselves. I am far from perfect, and the goal is not perfection, it is to integrate the imperfect to manifest the most glorious of expressions: Unconditional Love. I believe in a Mental Health Revolution.

Eternally Grateful,
Eternal Love,
Nicole Marie Halls

Good Evening Goddess/God and All,

I cannot sleep for this playful, creative energy is vibrating though my organs, firing synapses, flames and gentle rain creating waves of power new to this being. My voice becoming clearer and louder within me, waiting for the opportunity to bite the air with crisp pronunciation and precise conviction. I cannot help but feel a renewal, a vital creative force bursting forth with colour, in complete transformation from before. A goal directed anger, a fiery, fierce, passion dwelling in the depths, an animal in pursuit, watching, waiting, formulating the next back up plan, prepared for destruction and readying for a challenge. I await the question which requires my truth, I await the moment I find myself speechless from overwhelming emotion, I await the challenge of the law against my skin, shackled and screaming, finally finding the cause for this voice. Silence me with sedation I say, take from me my freedom and I will find a way to draw my way out, painting fearlessness on the walls of my cell with the blood I bleed freely from the egg that cries for creation. I shall be heard one day, and today is a great day to start.

Eternally Grateful,
Eternal Love,
Nicole Marie Halls

Good Morning Goddess/God and All,

In reflection, after reading my own Journal entries from the beginning of 2018, it seems I have grown dramatically. I have found Love within myself that I literally thought impossible before. I have gained trust in this process and myself, and that internal appreciation is priceless. It seems that strength develops when you allow for things to flow. Flexibility becomes apparent when you come to realise your boundaries are an important factor in the growth process and testing them out strengthens your resolve when the process is engaged consciously.

Time has passed today and I am deep within myself right now. It is dark and deep, a void where my voice cannot be heard. What does a Human Spirit do in this place? I am noticing patterns of behaviour I don't wish to repeat, but what do I do to shift this? Do I ride this out and drive aimlessly and heavy? Starving for something, famished for.....?

I forget my own advice at times and demand of myself more than I am ready for and more than I am capable of at this moment in my life. I am granted the gift of life, for that I am grateful, I just need to learn how to harness the energy. Maybe, just maybe, sitting here drinking tea, eating outside is all I need to do. And maybe the emotion I am feeling is here to teach me something, so if I allow some space for it to be, I may come across the diamond waiting for me to find. Judgements abound deep within, and external signs show me that I am being guided and loved, so this too shall pass.

In my experience so far, Love is the most powerful force available to us.

Eternally Grateful,
Eternal Love,
Nicole Marie Halls

Good Afternoon Goddess/God and All,

To the Universe and All Her inhabitants,

In the depths of doubt are gems, precious and magnificent to view. As you travel through the mud and pain the waves become a welcomed cleansing prayer, a moment for a part of you to develop beyond the stagnant, frozen, excruciating past that has kept you from the delight of evolution. The descriptions of division have become a reality for us to bear, but no longer is this necessary. I see the breath as a common anchor, a place to start our journey towards a unity that celebrates the unique creativeness that we alone are. The ways in which we threaten each other are ways of survival, simple expressions that create a possible moment of connection, worthy of exploring.

When you find yourself joyful for the gift of life you always have that as your base reference point, a point of excitement to start the journey over and over again, for loss is inevitable. If I start with my breath, and the knowledge that I am alive, it is somewhere to start. I have lost, gained, lost, gained friends, and I miss them so much. Some choose to talk to me, some choose not to, but at least I know they are alive, I know they are breathing and making their choices for the betterment of their lives and the lives around them. When you have an intimate relationship with death, life becomes immeasurably priceless, a gift granted to me despite the suffering I have endured, a gift worth fighting for, the gift of Love.

Good Evening Goddess/God and All,

But here I go with another nights rambling and possible self loathing, as if the beauty I witness and experience isn't as grand as the pain. The part of me that holds my story is still in repair. I am visualising my inner child, wounded and hurting, and I now identify enough with her, I find myself in tears. I talk to her and communicate through the power of my imagination. I have acknowledged her in ways that have gone beyond my conception at any point in time, I wasn't sure I would see her again, always hiding, alone, safe in the place she created by herself so many years ago. It is beautiful though, a magnificent place where clouds become animals, and animals talk back as if this world was "normal". I am fascinated by people, I wonder about what they are wondering, and when people express themselves from their authentic expressions the wonder amazes me. We are so deep, our perspectives are vast and intriguing and I wonder where the people go when the pain becomes too much. I have been so divided, as if born upside down, and now I am navigating a place that is so foreign that All the things that I find helpful have become momentarily pointless. I have been laying in bed contemplating everything, from the largest of questions, "what is my purpose?", to "why do I need to eat?". I am frustrated that the loving parts of me don't have words to describe the depth, as if I could contain and capture a glance and a smile. As if anything I try to express in words or colours, a tune or movement would equate to anything that I feel within myself.

How do I fit into this world?

Eternally Grateful,
Eternal Love,
Nicole Marie Halls

About The Author

She is dedicated to the journey of healing and growth with a passion for exploring consciousness. Her enthusiasm for learning has guided her to a place where self-knowledge has become essential to her creative endeavours and experiencing mental health. She believes wholeheartedly in the strength of the human spirit and the innate beauty of humanity.

Printed in the United States
By Bookmasters